Workshop on Integer Linear Programming for Natural Language Processing 2009

Held at NAACL HLT 2009

Boulder, Colorado, USA
4 June 2009

ISBN: 978-1-61738-563-6

Printed from e-media with permission by:

Curran Associates, Inc.
57 Morehouse Lane
Red Hook, NY 12571
www.proceedings.com

Some format issues inherent in the e-media version may also appear in this print version.

Printed by Curran Associates, Inc. (2010)

Association for Computational Linguistics
209 N. Eighth Street
Stroudsburg, Pennsylvania 18360

Phone: 1-570-476-8006
Fax: 1-570-476-0860

acl@aclweb.org

Introduction

We are pleased to present the proceedings of the Workshop on Integer Linear Programming for Natural Language Processing, held at NAACL HLT 2009 in Boulder, Colorado.

Integer Linear Programming (ILP) has recently attracted much attention within the NLP community. Formulating problems using ILP has several advantages. It allows us to focus on the modelling of problems, rather than engineering new search algorithms; provides the opportunity to incorporate generic global constraints; and guarantees exact inference. This and the availability of off-the-shelf solvers has led to a large variety of natural language processing tasks being formulated in the ILP framework, including semantic role labelling, syntactic parsing, summarisation and joint information extraction.

The use of ILP brings many benefits and opportunities but there are still challenges for the community; these include: formulations of new applications, dealing with large-scale problems and understanding the interaction between learning and inference at training and decision time. The purpose of this workshop was to bring together researchers interested in exploiting ILP for NLP applications and tackling the issues involved. We solicited full length papers, short papers and two-page abstracts with the purpose of providing a discussion on many topics.

We are grateful to the program committee for providing thoughtful and helpful reviews of the submitted papers. We also thank our invited speakers, Dan Roth, Andre Martins and Noah Smith for presenting their noteworthy work to the community.

We hope that you enjoy the workshop and these proceedings.

James Clarke
Sebastian Riedel

Organizers:

James Clarke, University of Illinois at Urbana-Champaign
Sebastian Riedel, University of Tokyo/DBCLS

Program Committee:

Ming-Wei Chang, University of Illinois at Urbana-Champaign
Hal Daume III, University of Utah
Pascal Denis, INRIA Paris-Rocquencourt
Mark Dras, Macquarie University
Katja Filippova, EML Research gGmbH
Jenny Rose Finkel, Stanford University
Manfred Klenner, University of Zurich
Kevin Knight, University of Southern California
Mirella Lapata, University of Edinburgh
Daniel Marcu, University of Southern California
Ryan McDonald, Google Research
Ivan Meza-Ruiz, University of Edinburgh
Nick Rizzolo, University of Illinois at Urbana-Champaign
Dan Roth, University of Illinois at Urbana-Champaign
Hiroya Takamura, Tokyo Institute of Technology
Scott Yih, Microsoft Research

Invited Speakers:

Andre Martins, Carnegie Mellon University
Dan Roth, University of Illinois at Urbana-Champaign
Noah Smith, Carnegie Mellon University

Table of Contents

Conference Program

Thursday, June 4, 2009

9:20–9:30	Opening Remarks
9:30–10:30	Invited Talk by Dan Roth
10:30–11:00	Coffee break
11:00–11:30	*Summarization with a Joint Model for Sentence Extraction and Compression* Andre Martins and Noah A. Smith
11:30–12:00	*A Scalable Global Model for Summarization* Dan Gillick and Benoit Favre
12:00–12:30	*Bounding and Comparing Methods for Correlation Clustering Beyond ILP* Micha Elsner and Warren Schudy
12:30–2:00	Lunch break
2:00–2:45	Invited Talk by Andre Martins and Noah Smith
2:45–3:15	*A New Objective Function for Word Alignment* Tugba Bodrumlu, Kevin Knight and Sujith Ravi
3:15–3:30	*A Constraint Programming Approach to Probabilistic Syntactic Processing* Irene Langkilde-Geary
3:30–4:00	Coffee break
4:00–5:00	Discussion

Summarization with a Joint Model for Sentence Extraction and Compression

André F. T. Martins[*†] and **Noah A. Smith**[*]
[*]School of Computer Science, Carnegie Mellon University, Pittsburgh, PA 15213, USA
[†]Instituto de Telecomunicações, Instituto Superior Técnico, Lisboa, Portugal
{afm,nasmith}@cs.cmu.edu

Abstract

Text summarization is one of the oldest problems in natural language processing. Popular approaches rely on extracting relevant sentences from the original documents. As a side effect, sentences that are too long but partly relevant are doomed to either not appear in the final summary, or prevent inclusion of other relevant sentences. Sentence compression is a recent framework that aims to select the shortest subsequence of words that yields an informative and grammatical sentence. This work proposes a one-step approach for document summarization that jointly performs sentence extraction and compression by solving an integer linear program. We report favorable experimental results on newswire data.

1 Introduction

Automatic text summarization dates back to the 1950s and 1960s (Luhn, 1958; Baxendale, 1958; Edmundson, 1969). Today, the proliferation of digital information makes research on summarization technologies more important than ever before. In the last two decades, machine learning techniques have been employed in **extractive summarization** of single documents (Kupiec et al., 1995; Aone et al., 1999; Osborne, 2002) and multiple documents (Radev and McKeown, 1998; Carbonell and Goldstein, 1998; Radev et al., 2000). Most of this work aims only to *extract* relevant sentences from the original documents and present them as the summary; this simplification of the problem yields scalable solutions.

Some attention has been devoted by the NLP community to the related problem of **sentence compression** (Knight and Marcu, 2000): given a long sentence, how to maximally *compress* it into a grammatical sentence that still preserves all the relevant information? While sentence compression is a promising framework with applications, for example, in headline generation (Dorr et al., 2003; Jin, 2003), little work has been done to include it as a module in document summarization systems. Most existing approaches (with some exceptions, like the vine-growth model of Daumé, 2006) use a two-stage architecture, either by first extracting a certain number of salient sentences and then feeding them into a sentence compressor, or by first compressing all sentences and extracting later. However, regardless of which operation is performed first—compression or extraction—two-step "pipeline" approaches may fail to find overall-optimal solutions; often the summaries are not better that the ones produced by extractive summarization. On the other hand, a pilot study carried out by Lin (2003) suggests that summarization systems that perform sentence compression have the potential to beat pure extractive systems if they model cross-sentence effects.

In this work, we address this issue by merging the tasks of sentence extraction and sentence compression into a *global* optimization problem. A careful design of the objective function encourages "sparse solutions," i.e., solutions that involve only a small number of sentences whose compressions are to be included in the summary. Our contributions are:

- We cast joint sentence extraction and compression as an integer linear program (ILP);
- We provide a new formulation of sentence compression using dependency parsing information that only requires a linear number of variables, and combine it with a bigram model;
- We show how the full model can be trained in a max-margin framework. Since a dataset of summaries comprised of extracted, compressed sentences is unavailable, we present a procedure that trains the compression and extraction models separately and tunes a parameter to interpolate the

Proceedings of the NAACL HLT Workshop on Integer Linear Programming for Natural Language Processing, pages 1–9,
Boulder, Colorado, June 2009.

two models.

The compression model and the full system are compared with state-of-the-art baselines in standard newswire datasets. This paper is organized as follows: §2–3 provide an overview of our two building blocks, sentence extraction and sentence compression. §4 describes our method to perform one-step sentence compression and extraction. §5 shows experiments in newswire data. Finally, §6 concludes the paper and suggests future work.

2 Extractive summarization

Extractive summarization builds a summary by extracting a few informative sentences from the documents. Let $D \triangleq \{t_1, \ldots, t_M\}$ be a set of sentences, contained in a single or in multiple related documents.[1] The goal is to extract the best sequence of sentences $\langle t_{i_1}, \ldots, t_{i_K} \rangle$ that summarizes D whose total length does not exceed a fixed budget of J words. We describe some well-known approaches that wil serve as our experimental baselines.

Extract the leading sentences (Lead). For single-document summarization, the simplest method consists of greedily extracting the leading sentences while they fit into the summary. A sentence is skipped if its inclusion exceeds the budget, and the next is examined. This performs extremely well in newswire articles, due to the journalistic convention of summarizing the article first.

Rank by relevance (Rel). This method ranks sentences by a relevance score, and then extracts the top ones that can fit into the summary. The score is typically a linear function of feature values:

$$\text{score}_{\text{rel}}(t_i) \triangleq \boldsymbol{\theta}^\top \mathbf{f}(t_i) = \textstyle\sum_{d=1}^{D} \theta_d f_d(t_i), \qquad (1)$$

Here, each $f_d(t_i)$ is a feature extracted from sentence t_i, and θ_d is the corresponding weight. In our experiments, relevance features include (i) the reciprocal position in the document, (ii) a binary feature indicating whether the sentence is the first one, and (iii) the 1-gram and 2-gram cosine similarity with the headline and with the full document.

[1] For simplicity, we describe a unified framework for single and multi-document summarization, although they may require specialized strategies. Here we experiment only with single-document summarization and assume $t_1, ..., t_M$ are ordered.

Maximal Marginal Relevance (MMR). For long documents or large collections, it becomes important to penalize the *redundancy* among the extracted sentences. Carbonell and Goldstein (1998) proposed greedily adding sentences to the summary S to maximize, at each step, a score of the form

$$\lambda \cdot \text{score}_{\text{rel}}(t_i) - (1-\lambda) \cdot \text{score}_{\text{red}}(t_i, S), \qquad (2)$$

where $\text{score}_{\text{rel}}(t_i)$ is as in Eq. 1 and $\text{score}_{\text{red}}(t_i, S)$ accounts for the *redundancy* between t_i and the current summary S. In our experiments, redundancy is the 1-gram cosine similarity between the sentence t_i and the current summary S. The trade-off between relevance and redundancy is controlled by $\lambda \in [0, 1]$, which is tuned on development data.

McDonald (2007) proposed a non-greedy variant of MMR that takes into account the redundancy between each pair of candidate sentences. This is cast as a global optimization problem:

$$\begin{aligned}\hat{S} &= \arg\max_{S} \lambda \cdot \textstyle\sum_{t_i \in S} \text{score}_{\text{rel}}(t_i) - \\ &\quad (1-\lambda) \cdot \textstyle\sum_{t_i, t_j \in S} \text{score}_{\text{red}}(t_i, t_j), \qquad (3)\end{aligned}$$

where $\text{score}_{\text{rel}}(t_i) \triangleq \boldsymbol{\theta}_{\text{rel}}^\top \mathbf{f}_{\text{rel}}(t_i)$, $\text{score}_{\text{red}}(t_i, t_j) \triangleq \boldsymbol{\theta}_{\text{red}}^\top \mathbf{f}_{\text{red}}(t_i, t_j)$, and $\mathbf{f}_{\text{rel}}(t_i)$ and $\mathbf{f}_{\text{red}}(t_i, t_j)$ are feature vectors with corresponding learned weight vectors $\boldsymbol{\theta}_{\text{rel}}$ and $\boldsymbol{\theta}_{\text{red}}$. He has shown how the relevance-based method and the MMR framework (in the non-greedy form of Eq. 3) can be cast as an ILP. By introducing indicator variables $\langle \mu_i \rangle_{i=1,\ldots,M}$ and $\langle \mu_{ij} \rangle_{i,j=1,\ldots,M}$ with the meanings

$$\begin{aligned}\mu_i &= \begin{cases} 1 & \text{if } t_i \text{ is to be extracted} \\ 0 & \text{otherwise} \end{cases} \\ \mu_{ij} &= \begin{cases} 1 & \text{if } t_i \text{ and } t_j \text{ are both to be extracted} \\ 0 & \text{otherwise} \end{cases}\end{aligned} \qquad (4)$$

one can reformulate Eq. 3 as an ILP with $O(M^2)$ variables and constraints:

$$\begin{aligned}\max_{\langle \mu_i \rangle, \langle \mu_{ij} \rangle} \quad & \lambda \cdot \textstyle\sum_{i=1}^{M} \mu_i \text{score}_{\text{rel}}(t_i) - \qquad (5) \\ & (1-\lambda) \cdot \textstyle\sum_{i=1}^{M} \sum_{j=1}^{M} \mu_{ij} \text{score}_{\text{red}}(t_i, t_j),\end{aligned}$$

subject to binary constraints $\mu_i, \mu_{ij} \in \{0, 1\}$, the length constraint $\sum_{i=1}^{M} \mu_i N_i \leq J$ (where N_i is the number of words of the ith sentence), and the following "agreement constraints" for $i, j = 1, \ldots, M$

(that impose the logical relation $\mu_{ij} = \mu_i \wedge \mu_j$):

$$\mu_{ij} \leq \mu_i, \quad \mu_{ij} \leq \mu_j, \quad \mu_{ij} \geq \mu_i + \mu_j - 1 \quad (6)$$

Let us provide a compact representation of the program in Eq. 5 that will be used later. Define our vector of parameters as $\boldsymbol{\theta} \triangleq [\lambda\boldsymbol{\theta}_{\text{rel}}, -(1-\lambda)\boldsymbol{\theta}_{\text{red}}]$. Packing all the feature vectors (one for each sentence, and one for each pair of sentences) into a matrix F,

$$\mathbf{F} \triangleq \begin{bmatrix} \mathbf{F}_{\text{rel}} & 0 \\ 0 & \mathbf{F}_{\text{red}} \end{bmatrix}, \quad (7)$$

with $\mathbf{F}_{\text{rel}} \triangleq [\mathbf{f}_{\text{rel}}(t_i)]_{1\leq i\leq M}$ and $\mathbf{F}_{\text{red}} \triangleq [\mathbf{f}_{\text{red}}(t_i, t_j)]_{1\leq i<j\leq M}$, and packing all the variables μ_i and μ_{ij} into a vector $\boldsymbol{\mu}$, the program in Eq. 5 can be compactly written as

$$\max_{\boldsymbol{\mu}} \boldsymbol{\theta}^\top \mathbf{F}\boldsymbol{\mu}, \quad (8)$$

subject to binary and linear constraints on $\boldsymbol{\mu}$. This formulation requires $O(M^2)$ variables and constraints. If we do not penalize sentence redundancy, the redundancy term may be dropped; in this simpler case, $\mathbf{F} = \mathbf{F}_{\text{rel}}$, the vector $\boldsymbol{\mu}$ only contains the variables $\langle\mu_i\rangle$, and the program in Eq. 8 only requires $O(M)$ variables and constraints. Our method (to be presented in §4) will build on this latter formulation.

3 Sentence Compression

Despite its simplicity, extractive summarization has a few shortcomings: for example, if the original sentences are too long or embed several clauses, there is no way of preventing lengthy sentences from appearing in the final summary. The **sentence compression** framework (Knight and Marcu, 2000) aims to select the best *subsequence* of words that still yields a short, informative and grammatical sentence. Such a sentence compressor is given a sentence $t \triangleq \langle w_1, \ldots, w_N\rangle$ as input and outputs a subsequence of length L, $c \triangleq \langle w_{j_1}, \ldots, w_{j_L}\rangle$, with $1 \leq j_1 < \ldots < j_L \leq N$. We may represent this output as a binary vector s of length N, where $s_j = 1$ iff word w_j is included in the compression. Note that there are $O(2^N)$ possible subsequences.

3.1 Related Work

Past approaches to sentence compression include a noisy channel formulation (Knight and Marcu, 2000; Daumé and Marcu, 2002), heuristic methods that parse the sentence and then trim constituents according to linguistic criteria (Dorr et al., 2003; Zajic et al., 2006), a pure discriminative model (McDonald, 2006), and an ILP formulation (Clarke and Lapata, 2008). We next give an overview of the two latter approaches.

McDonald (2006) uses the outputs of two parsers (a phrase-based and a dependency parser) as features in a discriminative model that decomposes over pairs of consecutive words. Formally, given a sentence $t = \langle w_1, \ldots, w_N\rangle$, the score of a compression $c = \langle w_{j_1}, \ldots, w_{j_L}\rangle$ decomposes as:

$$\text{score}(c; t) = \textstyle\sum_{l=2}^{L} \boldsymbol{\theta}^\top \mathbf{f}(t, j_{l-1}, j_l) \quad (9)$$

where $\mathbf{f}(t, j_{l-1}, j_l)$ are feature vectors that depend on the original sentence t and consecutive positions j_{l-1} and j_l, and $\boldsymbol{\theta}$ is a learned weight vector. The factorization in Eq. 9 allows exact decoding with dynamic programming.

Clarke and Lapata (2008) cast the problem as an ILP. In their formulation, Eq. 9 may be expressed as:

$$\begin{aligned}\text{score}(c; t) \quad = \quad & \sum_{i=1}^{N} \alpha_i \boldsymbol{\theta}^\top \mathbf{f}(t, 0, i) + \\ & \sum_{i=1}^{N} \beta_i \boldsymbol{\theta}^\top \mathbf{f}(t, i, n+1) + \\ & \sum_{i=1}^{N-1} \sum_{j=i+1}^{N} \gamma_{ij} \boldsymbol{\theta}^\top \mathbf{f}(t, i, j), \quad (10)\end{aligned}$$

where α_i, β_i, and γ_{ij} are additional binary variables with the following meanings:

- $\alpha_i = 1$ iff word w_i starts the compression;
- $\beta_i = 1$ iff word w_i ends the compression;
- $\gamma_{ij} = 1$ iff words w_i and w_j appear consecutively in the compression;

and subject to the following agreement constraints:

$$\begin{aligned}\textstyle\sum_{i=1}^{N} \alpha_i &= 1 \\ \textstyle\sum_{i=1}^{N} \beta_i &= 1 \\ s_j &= \alpha_j + \textstyle\sum_{i=1}^{j-1} \gamma_{ij} \\ s_i &= \beta_i + \textstyle\sum_{j=i+1}^{N} \gamma_{ij}. \quad (11)\end{aligned}$$

This framework also allows the inclusion of constraints to enforce grammaticality.

To compress a sentence, one needs to maximize the score in Eq. 10 subject to the constraints in Eq. 11. Representing the variables through

$$\boldsymbol{\nu} \triangleq \langle \alpha_1, \ldots, \alpha_N, \beta_1, \ldots, \beta_N, \gamma_{11}, \ldots, \gamma_{NN} \rangle \quad (12)$$

and packing the feature vectors into a matrix F, we obtain the ILP

$$\max_{\mathbf{s},\boldsymbol{\nu}} \boldsymbol{\theta}^\top \mathbf{F} \boldsymbol{\nu} \quad (13)$$

subject to linear and integer constraints on the variables s and $\boldsymbol{\nu}$. This particular formulation requires $O(N^2)$ variables and constraints.

3.2 Proposed Method

We propose an alternative model for sentence compression that may be formulated as an ILP, as in Eq. 13, but with only $O(N)$ variables and constraints. This formulation is based on the output of a dependency parser.

Directed arcs in a dependency tree link pairs of words, namely a *head* to its *modifier*. A dependency parse tree is characterized by a set of labeled arcs of the form (head, modifier, label); see Fig.1 for an example. Given a sentence $t = \langle w_1, \ldots, w_N \rangle$, we write $i = \pi(j)$ to denote that the ith word is the head (the "parent") of the jth word; if j is the root, we write $\pi(j) = 0$. Let s be the binary vector de-

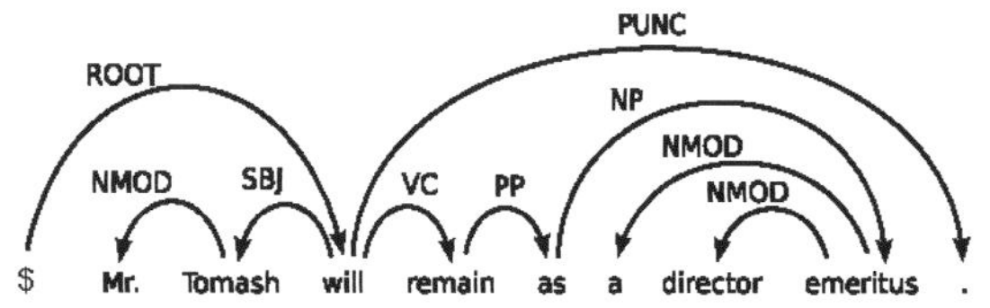

Figure 1: A dependency parse for an English sentence; example from McDonald and Satta (2007).

scribing a possible compression c for the sentence t. For each word j, we consider four possible cases, accounting for the inclusion or not of j and $\pi(j)$ in the compression. We introduce (mutually exclusive) binary variables ν_{j11}, ν_{j10}, ν_{j01}, and ν_{j00} to indicate each of these cases, i.e., for $a, b \in \{0, 1\}$,

$$\nu_{jab} \triangleq s_j = a \wedge s_{\pi(j)} = b. \quad (14)$$

Consider feature vectors $\mathbf{f}_{11}(t, j)$, $\mathbf{f}_{10}(t, j)$, $\mathbf{f}_{01}(t, j)$, and $\mathbf{f}_{00}(t, j)$, that look at the surface sentence and at the status of the word j and its head $\pi(j)$; these features have corresponding weight vectors $\boldsymbol{\theta}_{11}$, $\boldsymbol{\theta}_{10}$, $\boldsymbol{\theta}_{01}$, and $\boldsymbol{\theta}_{00}$. The score of c is written as:

$$\begin{aligned} \text{score}(c; t) &= \textstyle\sum_{j=1}^{N} \sum_{a,b \in \{0,1\}} \nu_{jab} \boldsymbol{\theta}_{ab}^\top \mathbf{f}_{ab}(t, j) \\ &= \textstyle\sum_{a,b \in \{0,1\}} \boldsymbol{\theta}_{ab}^\top \mathbf{F}_{ab} \boldsymbol{\nu}_{ab} \\ &= \boldsymbol{\theta}^\top \mathbf{F} \boldsymbol{\nu}, \end{aligned} \quad (15)$$

where $\mathbf{F}_{ab} \triangleq [\mathbf{f}_{ab}(t, 1), \ldots, \mathbf{f}_{ab}(t, N)]$, $\boldsymbol{\nu}_{ab} \triangleq (\nu_{jab})_{j=1,\ldots,N}$, $\boldsymbol{\theta} \triangleq (\boldsymbol{\theta}_{11}, \boldsymbol{\theta}_{10}, \boldsymbol{\theta}_{01}, \boldsymbol{\theta}_{00})$, and $\mathbf{F} \triangleq \text{Diag}(\mathbf{F}_{11}, \mathbf{F}_{10}, \mathbf{F}_{01}, \mathbf{F}_{00})$ (a block-diagonal matrix).

We have reached in Eq. 15 an ILP isomorphic to the one in Eq. 13, but only with $O(N)$ variables. There are some agreement constraints between the variables $\boldsymbol{\nu}$ and s that reflect the logical relations in Eq. 14; these may be written as linear inequalities (cf. Eq. 6), yielding $O(N)$ constraints.

Given this proposal and §3.1, it is also straightforward to extend this model to include bigram features as in Eq. 10; the combination of dependency relation features and bigram features yields a model that is more powerful than both models in Eq. 15 and Eq. 10. Such a model is expressible as an ILP with $O(N^2)$ variables and constraints, making use of the variables s, $\boldsymbol{\nu}$, $\boldsymbol{\alpha}$, $\boldsymbol{\beta}$ and $\boldsymbol{\gamma}$. In §5, we compare the performance of this model (called "Bigram") and the model in Eq. 15 (called "NoBigram").[2]

4 Joint Compression and Extraction

We next describe our joint model for sentence compression and extraction. Let $D \triangleq \{t_1, \ldots, t_M\}$ be a set of sentences as in §2, each expressed as a sequence of words, $t_i \triangleq \langle w_{i1}, \ldots, w_{iN_i} \rangle$. Following §3, we represent a *compression* of t_i as a binary vector $\mathbf{s}_i = \langle s_{i1}, \ldots, s_{iN_i} \rangle$, where $s_{ij} = 1$ iff word w_{ij}

[2] It should be noted that more efficient decoders are possible that do not require solving an ILP. In particular, inference in the NoBigram variant can performed in polynomial time with dynamic programming algorithms that propagate messages along the dependency parse tree; for the Bigram variant, dynamic programming can still be employed with some additional storage. Our ILP formulation, however, is more suited to the final goal of performing document summarization (of which our sentence compression model will be a component); furthermore, it also allows the straightforward inclusion of global linguistic constraints, which, as shown by Clarke and Lapata (2008), can greatly improve the grammaticality of the compressions.

is included in the compression. Now, define a *summary* of D as a set of sentences obtained by *extracting* and *compressing* sentences from D. More precisely, let $\mu_1, \ldots, \mu_M$ be binary variables, one for each sentence t_i in D; define $\mu_i = 1$ iff a compression of sentence t_i is used in the summary. A summary of D is then represented by the binary variables $\langle \mu_1, \ldots, \mu_M, \mathbf{s}_1, \ldots, \mathbf{s}_M \rangle$. Notice that these variables are redundant:

$$\mu_i = 0 \quad \Leftrightarrow \quad \forall j \in \{1, \ldots, N_i\} \quad s_{ij} = 0, \quad (16)$$

i.e., an empty compression means that the sentence is not to be extracted. In the sequel, it will become clear why this redundancy is convenient.

Most approaches up to now are concerned with either *extraction* or *compression*, not both at the same time. We will combine the extraction scores in Eq. 8 and the compression scores in Eq. 15 to obtain a single, global optimization problem;[3] we rename the extraction features and parameters to $\mathbf{F}_e$ and $\boldsymbol{\theta}_e$ and the compression features and parameters to $\mathbf{F}_c$ and $\boldsymbol{\theta}_c$:

$$\max_{\boldsymbol{\mu}, \boldsymbol{\nu}, \mathbf{s}} \boldsymbol{\theta}_e^T \mathbf{F}_e \boldsymbol{\mu} + \textstyle\sum_{i=1}^M \boldsymbol{\theta}_c^T \mathbf{F}_{ci} \boldsymbol{\nu}_i, \quad (17)$$

subject to agreement constraints on the variables $\boldsymbol{\nu}_i$ and $\mathbf{s}_i$ (see Eqs. 11 and 14), and new agreement constraints on the variables $\boldsymbol{\mu}$ and $\mathbf{s}_1, \ldots, \mathbf{s}_M$ to enforce the relation in Eq. 16:

$$\begin{array}{rcl} s_{ij} & \leq & \mu_i, \quad \forall i = 1, \ldots, M, \forall j = 1, \ldots, N_i \\ \mu_i & \leq & \sum_{j=1}^{N_i} s_{ij}, \quad \forall i = 1, \ldots, M \end{array} \quad (18)$$

The constraint that the length of the summary cannot exceed J words is encoded as:

$$\textstyle\sum_{i=1}^M \sum_{j=1}^{N_i} s_{ij} \leq J. \quad (19)$$

All variables are further restricted to be binary. We also want to avoid picking just a few words from many sentences, which typically leads to ungrammatical summaries. Hence it is desirable to obtain "sparse" solutions with only a few sentences extracted and compressed (and most components of $\boldsymbol{\mu}$ are zero) To do so, we add the constraint

$$\textstyle\sum_{j=1}^{N_i} s_{ij} \geq \mu_i \rho N_i, \quad i = 1, \ldots, M, \quad (20)$$

which states, for each sentence t_i, that t_i should be ignored or have at least ρN_i words extracted. We fix $\rho = 0.8$, enforcing compression rates below 80%.[4]

To learn the model parameters $\boldsymbol{\theta} = \langle \boldsymbol{\theta}_e, \boldsymbol{\theta}_c \rangle$, we can use a max-margin discriminative learning algorithm like MIRA (Crammer and Singer, 2003), which is quite effective and scalable. However, there is not (to our knowledge) a single dataset of extracted *and* compressed sentences. Instead, as will be described in Sec. 5.1, there are separate datasets of extracted sentences, and datasets of compressed sentences. Therefore, instead of globally learning the model parameters, $\boldsymbol{\theta} = \langle \boldsymbol{\theta}_e, \boldsymbol{\theta}_c \rangle$, we propose the following strategy to learn them separately:

- Learn $\boldsymbol{\theta}'_e$ using a corpus of extracted sentences,
- Learn $\boldsymbol{\theta}'_c$ using a corpus of compressed sentences,
- Tune η so that $\boldsymbol{\theta} = \langle \boldsymbol{\theta}'_e, \eta \boldsymbol{\theta}'_c \rangle$ has good performance on development data. (This is necessary since each set of weights is learned up to scaling.)

5 Experiments

5.1 Datasets, Evaluation and Environment

For our experiments, two datasets were used:

The DUC 2002 dataset. This is a collection of newswire articles, comprised of 59 document clusters. Each document within the collections (out of a total of 567 documents) has one or two manually created abstracts with approximately 100 words.[5]

Clarke's dataset for sentence compression. This is the dataset used by Clarke and Lapata (2008). It contains manually created compressions of 82 newspaper articles (1,433 sentences) from the British National Corpus and the American News Text corpus.[6]

To evaluate the sentence compressor alone, we measured the compression rate and the precision, recall, and F_1-measure (both macro and micro-averaged) with respect to the "gold" compressed

[3] In what follows, we use the formulation in Eq. 8 *without* the redundancy terms; however these can be included in a straightforward way, naturally increasing the number of variables/constraints.

[4] There are alternative ways to achieve "sparseness," either in a soft way, by adding a term $-\lambda \sum_i \mu_i$ to the objective, or using a different hard constraint, like $\sum_i \mu_i \leq K$, to limit the number of sentences from which to pick words.

[5] http://duc.nist.gov

[6] http://homepages.inf.ed.ac.uk/s0460084/data

	Compression Ratio	Micro-Av. P	Micro-Av. R	Micro-Av. F_1	Macro-Av. P	Macro-Av. R	Macro-Av. F_1
HedgeTrimmer	57.64%	0.7099	0.5925	0.6459	0.7195	0.6547	0.6367
McDonald (2006)	71.40%	0.7444	0.7697	0.7568	0.7711	0.7852	**0.7696**
NoBigram	71.20%	0.7399	0.7626	0.7510	0.7645	0.7730	**0.7604**
Bigram	71.35%	0.7472	0.7720	0.7594	0.7737	0.7848	**0.7710**

Table 1: Results for sentence compression in the Clarke's test dataset (441 sentences) for our implementation of the baseline systems (*HedgeTrimmer* and the system described in McDonald, 2006), and the two variants of our model, NoBigram and Bigram. The compression ratio associated with the reference compressed sentences in this dataset is 69.06%. In the rightmost column, the statistically indistinguishable best results are emboldened, based on a paired t-test applied to the sequence of F_1 measures ($p < 0.01$).

sentences, calculated on unigrams.[7]

To evaluate the full system, we used Rouge-N (Lin and Hovy, 2002), a popular n-gram recall-based automatic evaluation measure. This score compares the summary produced by a system with one or more valid reference summaries.

All our experiments were conducted on a PC with a Intel dual-core processor with 2.66 GHz and 2 Gb RAM memory. We used ILOG CPLEX, a commercial integer programming solver. The interface with CPLEX was coded in Java.

5.2 Sentence Compression

We split Clarke's dataset into two partitions, one used for training (1,188 sentences) and the other for testing (441 sentences). This dataset includes one manual compression for each sentence, that we use as reference for evaluation purposes. Compression ratio, i.e., the fraction of words included in the compressed sentences, is 69.32% (micro-averaged over the training partition).

For comparison, two baselines were implemented: a simple compressor based on Hedge Trimmer, the headline generation system of Dorr et al. (2003) and Zajic et al. (2006),[8] and the discriminative model described by McDonald (2006), which captures "soft syntactic evidence" (we reproduced the same set of features). Both systems require a phrase-structure parser; we used Collins' parser (Collins, 1999);[9] the latter system also derives features from a dependency parser; we used the MST-Parser (McDonald et al., 2005).[10]

We implemented the two variants of our compressor described in §3.2.

NoBigram. This variant factors the compression score as a sum over individual scores, each depending on the inclusion or not of each word and its head in the compression (see Eq. 15). An upper bound of 70% was placed on the compression ratio. As stated in §3.2, inference amounts to solving an ILP with $O(N)$ variables and constraints, N being the sentence length. We also used MSTParser to obtain the dependency parse trees.

Bigram. This variant includes an extra term standing for a *bigram score*, which factors as a sum over pairs of consecutive words. As in McDonald (2006), we include features that depend on the "in-between" words in the original sentence that are to be omitted in the compression.[11] As stated in §3.2, inference through this model can be done by solving an ILP with $O(N^2)$ variables and constraints.

[7] Notice that this evaluation score is not able to properly capture the grammaticality of the compression; this is a known issue that typically is addressed by requiring human judgments.

[8] Hedge Trimmer applies a deterministic compression procedure whose first step is to identify the lowest leftmost `S` node in the parse tree that contains a `NP` and a `VP`; this node is taken as the root of the compressed sentence (i.e., all words that are not spanned by this node are discarded). Further steps described by Dorr et al. (2003) include removal of low content units, and an "iterative shortening" loop that keeps removing constituents until a desired compression ratio is achieved. The best results were obtained without iterative shortening, which is explained by the fact that the selection of the lowest leftmost `S` node (first step of the algorithm) already provides significant compression, as illustrated in Table 1.

[9] `http://people.csail.mit.edu/mcollins/code.html`

[10] `http://sourceforge.net/projects/mstparser`

[11] The major difference between this variant and model of McDonald (2006) is that the latter employs "soft syntactic evidence" as *input* features, while we make the dependency relations part of the *output* features. All the non-syntactic features are the same. Apart from this, notice that our variant does not employ a phrase-structure parser.

For both variants, we used MSTParser to obtain the dependency parse trees. The model parameters are learned in a pure discriminative way through a max-margin approach. We used the 1-best MIRA algorithm (Crammer and Singer, 2003; McDonald et al., 2005) for training; this is a fast online algorithm that requires solving the inference problem at each step. Although inference amounts to solving an ILP, which in the worst case scales exponentially with the size of the sentence, training the model is in practice very fast for the NoBigram model (a few minutes in the environment described in §5.1) and fast enough for the Bigram model (a couple of hours using the same equipment). This is explained by the fact that sentences don't usually exceed a few tens of words, and because of the structure of the ILPs, whose constraint matrices are very sparse.

Table 1 depicts the micro- and macro-averaged precision, recall and F_1-measure. We can see that both variants outperform the Hedge Trimmer baseline by a great margin, and are in line with the system of McDonald (2006); however, none of our variants employ a phrase-structure parser. We also observe that our simpler NoBigram variant, which uses a linear-sized ILP, achieves results similar to these two systems.

5.3 Joint Compression and Extraction

For the summarization task, we split the DUC 2002 dataset into a training partition (427 documents) and a testing partition (140 documents). The training partition was further split into a training and a development set. We evaluated the performance of Lead, Rel, and MMR as baselines (all are described in §2). Weights for Rel were learned via the SVM-Rank algorithm;[12] to create a gold-standard ranking, we sorted the sentences by Rouge-2 score[13] (with respect to the human created summaries). We include a Pipeline baseline as well, which ranks all sentences by relevance, then includes their compressions (using the Bigram variant) while they fit into the summary.

We tested two variants of our joint model, combining the Rel extraction model with (i) the NoBigram compression model (§3.2) and (ii) the Bigram variant. Each variant was trained with the procedure described in §4. To keep tractability, the inference ILP problem was relaxed (the binary constraints were relaxed to unit interval constraints) and non-integer solution values were rounded to produce a valid summary, both for training and testing.[14] Whenever this procedure yielded a summary longer than 100 words, we truncated it to fit the word limit.

	Rouge-1	Rouge-2
Lead	0.384 ± 0.080	$\mathbf{0.177 \pm 0.083}$
Rel	0.389 ± 0.074	$\mathbf{0.178 \pm 0.080}$
MMR $\lambda = 0.25$	0.392 ± 0.071	$\mathbf{0.178 \pm 0.077}$
Pipeline	0.380 ± 0.073	0.173 ± 0.073
Rel + NoBigr $\eta = 1.5$	$\mathbf{0.403 \pm 0.080}$	$\mathbf{0.180 \pm 0.082}$
Rel + Bigr $\eta = 4.0$	$\mathbf{0.403 \pm 0.076}$	$\mathbf{0.180 \pm 0.076}$

Table 2: Results for sentence extraction in the DUC2002 dataset (140 documents). Bold indicates the best results with statistical significance, according to a paired t-test ($p < 0.01$); Rouge-2 scores of all systems except Pipeline are indistinguishable according to the same test, with $p > 0.05$.

Table 2 depicts the results of each of the above systems in terms of Rouge-1 and Rouge-2 scores. We can see that both variants of our system are able to achieve the best results in terms of Rouge-1 and Rouge-2 scores. The suboptimality of extracting and compressing in separate stages is clear from the table, as Pipeline performs worse than the pure extractive systems. We also note that the configuration Rel + Bigram is not able to outperform Rel + NoBigram, despite being computationally more expensive (about 25 minutes to process the whole test set, against the 7 minutes taken by the Rel + NoBigram variant). Fig. 2 exemplifies the summaries produced by our system. We see that both variants were able to include new pieces of information in the summary without sacrificing grammaticality.

These results suggest that our system, being capable of performing joint sentence extraction and compression to summarize a document, offers a powerful alternative to pure extractive systems. Finally, we note that no labeled datasets currently exist on which our full model could have been trained with supervision; therefore, although inference is performed

[12]SVMRank is implemented in the SVM^{light} toolkit (Joachims, 1999), `http://svmlight.joachims.org`.

[13]A similar system was implemented that optimizes the Rouge-1 score instead, but it led to inferior performance.

[14]See Martins et al. (2009) for a study concerning the impact of LP relaxations in the learning problem.

MMR baseline:

Australian novelist Peter Carey was awarded the coveted Booker Prize for fiction Tuesday night for his love story, "Oscar and Lucinda".

A panel of five judges unanimously announced the award of the $26,250 prize after an 80-minute deliberation during a banquet at London's ancient Guildhall.

Carey, who lives in Sydney with his wife and son, said in a brief speech that like the other five finalists he had been asked to attend with a short speech in his pocket in case he won.

Rel + NoBigram:

Australian novelist Peter Carey was awarded the *coveted* Booker Prize for fiction *Tuesday night* for his love story, "Oscar and Lucinda".

A panel of five judges *unanimously* announced the award of the $26,250 prize after an *80-minute* deliberation during a banquet at London's ancient Guildhall.

The judges made their selection from 102 books published in Britain in the past 12 months *and which they read in their homes.*

Carey, who lives in Sydney with his wife and son, said *in a brief speech that* like the other five finalists he had been asked to attend with a short speech in his pocket in case he won.

Rel + Bigram:

Australian novelist Peter Carey was awarded the *coveted* Booker Prize for fiction *Tuesday night* for his *love* story, "Oscar and Lucinda".

A panel of *five* judges *unanimously* announced the award of the $26,250 prize after an *80-minute* deliberation during a banquet at London's ancient Guildhall.

He was unsuccessful in the prize competition in 1985 when his novel, "Illywhacker," was among the final six.

Carey called the award a "*great* honor" and he thanked the prize sponsors for "provoking *so much* passionate discussion *about literature* *– perhaps* there will be *more* tomorrow".

Carey was the *only* non-Briton in the final six.

Figure 2: Summaries produced by the strongest baseline (MMR) and the two variants of our system. Deleted words are *marked as such.*

jointly, our training procedure had to learn separately the extraction and the compression models, and to tune a scalar parameter to trade off the two models. We conjecture that a better model could have been learned if a labeled dataset with extracted compressed sentences existed.

6 Conclusion and Future Work

We have presented a summarization system that performs sentence extraction and compression in a single step, by casting the problem as an ILP. The summary optimizes an objective function that includes both extraction and compression scores. Our model encourages "sparse" summaries that involve only a few sentences. Experiments in newswire data suggest that our system is a valid alternative to existing extraction-based systems. However, it is worth noting that further evaluation (e.g., human judgments) needs to be carried out to assert the quality of our summaries, e.g., their grammaticality, something that the Rouge scores cannot fully capture.

Future work will address the possibility of including linguistic features and constraints to further improve the grammaticality of the produced summaries.

Another straightforward extension is the inclusion of a redundancy term and a query relevance term in the objective function. For redundancy, a similar idea of that of McDonald (2007) can be applied, yielding a ILP with $O(M^2 + N)$ variables and constraints (M being the number of sentences and N the total number of words). However, such model will take into account the redundancy among the original sentences and not their compressions; to model the redundancy accross compressions, a possibility is to consider a linear redundancy score (similar to cosine similarity, but without the normalization), which would result in an ILP with $O(N + \sum_i P_i^2)$ variables and constraints, where $P_i \leq M$ is the number of sentences in which word w_i occurs; this is no worse than $O(M^2 N)$.

We also intend to model discourse, which, as shown by Daumé and Marcu (2002), plays an important role in document summarization. Another future direction is to extend our ILP formulations to more sophisticated models that go beyond word deletion, like the ones proposed by Cohn and Lapata (2008).

Acknowledgments

The authors thank the anonymous reviewers for helpful comments, Yiming Yang for interesting discussions, and Dipanjan Das and Sourish Chaudhuri for providing their code. This research was supported by a grant from FCT through the CMU-Portugal Program and the Information and Communications Technologies Institute (ICTI) at CMU, and also by Priberam Informática.

References

C. Aone, M. E. Okurowski, J. Gorlinsky, and B. Larsen. 1999. A trainable summarizer with knowledge acquired from robust nlp techniques. In *Advances in Automatic Text Summarization*. MIT Press.

P. B. Baxendale. 1958. Machine-made index for technical literature—an experiment. *IBM Journal of Research Development*, 2(4):354–361.

J. Carbonell and J. Goldstein. 1998. The use of MMR, diversity-based reranking for reordering documents and producing summaries. In *Proc. of SIGIR*.

J. Clarke and M. Lapata. 2008. Global inference for sentence compression an integer linear programming approach. *JAIR*, 31:399–429.

T. Cohn and M. Lapata. 2008. Sentence compression beyond word deletion. In *Proc. COLING*.

M. Collins. 1999. *Head-Driven Statistical Models for Natural Language Parsing*. Ph.D. thesis, University of Pennsylvania.

K. Crammer and Yoram Singer. 2003. Ultraconservative online algorithms for multiclass problems. *J. Mach. Learn. Res.*, 3:951–991.

H. Daumé and D. Marcu. 2002. A noisy-channel model for document compression. In *Proc. of ACL*.

H. Daumé. 2006. *Practical Structured Learning Techniques for Natural Language Processing*. Ph.D. thesis, University of Southern California.

B. Dorr, D. Zajic, and R. Schwartz. 2003. Hedge trimmer: A parse-and-trim approach to headline generation. In *Proc. of HLT-NAACL Text Summarization Workshop and DUC*.

H. P. Edmundson. 1969. New methods in automatic extracting. *Journal of the ACM*, 16(2):264–285.

R. Jin. 2003. *Statistical Approaches Toward Title Generation*. Ph.D. thesis, Carnegie Mellon University.

T. Joachims. 1999. Making large-scale SVM learning practical. In *Advances in Kernel Methods - Support Vector Learning*. MIT Press.

K. Knight and D. Marcu. 2000. Statistics-based summarization—step one: Sentence compression. In *Proc. of AAAI/IAAI*.

J. Kupiec, J. Pedersen, and F. Chen. 1995. A trainable document summarizer. In *Proc. of SIGIR*.

C.-Y. Lin and E. Hovy. 2002. Manual and automatic evaluation of summaries. In *Proc. of the ACL Workshop on Automatic Summarization*.

C.-Y. Lin. 2003. Improving summarization performance by sentence compression-a pilot study. In *Proc. of the Int. Workshop on Inf. Ret. with Asian Languages*.

H. P. Luhn. 1958. The automatic creation of literature abstracts. *IBM Journal of Research Development*, 2(2):159–165.

A. F. T. Martins, N. A. Smith, and E. P. Xing. 2009. Polyhedral outer approximations with application to natural language parsing. In *Proc. of ICML*.

R. T. McDonald, F. Pereira, K. Ribarov, and J. Hajič. 2005. Non-projective dependency parsing using spanning tree algorithms. In *Proc. of HLT-EMNLP*.

R. McDonald. 2006. Discriminative sentence compression with soft syntactic constraints. In *Proc. of EACL*.

R. McDonald. 2007. A study of global inference algorithms in multi-document summarization. In *Proc. of ECIR*.

M. Osborne. 2002. Using maximum entropy for sentence extraction. In *Proc. of the ACL Workshop on Automatic Summarization*.

D. R. Radev and K. McKeown. 1998. Generating natural language summaries from multiple on-line sources. *Computational Linguistics*, 24(3):469–500.

D. R. Radev, H. Jing, and M. Budzikowska. 2000. Centroid-based summarization of multiple documents: sentence extraction, utility-based evaluation, and user studies. In *Proc. of the NAACL-ANLP Workshop on Automatic Summarization*.

D. Zajic, B. Dorr, J. Lin, and R. Schwartz. 2006. Sentence compression as a component of a multi-document summarization system. In *Proc. of the ACL DUC Workshop*.

A Scalable Global Model for Summarization

Dan Gillick[1,2], **Benoit Favre**[2]
[1] Computer Science Division, University of California Berkeley, USA
[2] International Computer Science Institute, Berkeley, USA
{dgillick,favre}@icsi.berkeley.edu

Abstract

We present an Integer Linear Program for exact inference under a maximum coverage model for automatic summarization. We compare our model, which operates at the sub-sentence or "concept"-level, to a sentence-level model, previously solved with an ILP. Our model scales more efficiently to larger problems because it does not require a quadratic number of variables to address redundancy in pairs of selected sentences. We also show how to include sentence compression in the ILP formulation, which has the desirable property of performing compression and sentence selection simultaneously. The resulting system performs at least as well as the best systems participating in the recent Text Analysis Conference, as judged by a variety of automatic and manual content-based metrics.

1 Introduction

Automatic summarization systems are typically extractive or abstractive. Since abstraction is quite hard, the most successful systems tested at the Text Analysis Conference (TAC) and Document Understanding Conference (DUC)[1], for example, are extractive. In particular, sentence selection represents a reasonable trade-off between linguistic quality, guaranteed by longer textual units, and summary content, often improved with shorter units.

Whereas the majority of approaches employ a greedy search to find a set of sentences that is both relevant and non-redundant (Goldstein et al., 2000; Nenkova and Vanderwende, 2005), some recent work focuses on improved search (McDonald, 2007; Yih et al., 2007). Among them, McDonald is the first to consider a non-approximated maximization of an objective function through Integer Linear Programming (ILP), which improves on a greedy search by 4-12%. His formulation assumes that the quality of a summary is proportional to the sum of the relevance scores of the selected sentences, penalized by the sum of the redundancy scores of all pairs of selected sentences. Under a maximum summary length constraint, this problem can be expressed as a quadratic knapsack (Gallo et al., 1980) and many methods are available to solve it (Pisinger et al., 2005). However, McDonald reports that the method is not scalable above 100 input sentences and discusses more practical approximations. Still, an ILP formulation is appealing because it gives exact solutions and lends itself well to extensions through additional constraints.

Methods like McDonald's, including the well-known Maximal Marginal Relevance (MMR) algorithm (Goldstein et al., 2000), are subject to another problem: Summary-level redundancy is not always well modeled by pairwise sentence-level redundancy. Figure 1 shows an example where the combination of sentences (1) and (2) overlaps completely with sentence (3), a fact not captured by pairwise redundancy measures. Redundancy, like content selection, is a global problem.

Here, we discuss a model for sentence selection with a globally optimal solution that also addresses redundancy globally. We choose to represent infor-

[1] TAC is a continuation of DUC, which ran from 2001-2007.

Proceedings of the NAACL HLT Workshop on Integer Linear Programming for Natural Language Processing, pages 10–18,
Boulder, Colorado, June 2009.

(1) The cat is in the kitchen.
(2) The cat drinks the milk.
(3) The cat drinks the milk in the kitchen.

Figure 1: Example of sentences redundant as a group. Their redundancy is only partially captured by sentence-level pairwise measurement.

mation at a finer granularity than sentences, with concepts, and assume that the value of a summary is the sum of the values of the unique concepts it contains. While the concepts we use in experiments are word n-grams, we use the generic term to emphasize that this is just one possible definition. Only crediting each concept once serves as an implicit global constraint on redundancy. We show how the resulting optimization problem can be mapped to an ILP that can be solved efficiently with standard software.

We begin by comparing our model to McDonald's (section 2) and detail the differences between the resulting ILP formulations (section 3), showing that ours can give competitive results (section 4) and offer better scalability[2] (section 5). Next we demonstrate how our ILP formulation can be extended to include efficient parse-tree-based sentence compression (section 6). We review related work (section 7) and conclude with a discussion of potential improvements to the model (section 8).

2 Models

The model proposed by McDonald (2007) considers information and redundancy at the sentence level. The score of a summary is defined as the sum of the relevance scores of the sentences it contains minus the sum of the redundancy scores of each pair of these sentences. If s_i is an indicator for the presence of sentence i in the summary, Rel_i is its relevance, and Red_{ij} is its redundancy with sentence j, then a summary is scored according to:

$$\sum_i Rel_i s_i - \sum_{ij} Red_{ij} s_i s_j$$

Generating a summary under this model involves maximizing this objective function, subject to a length constraint. A variety of choices for Rel_i and Red_{ij} are possible, from simple word overlap metrics to the output of feature-based classifiers trained to perform information retrieval and textual entailment.

As an alternative, we consider information and redundancy at a sub-sentence, "concept" level, modeling the value of a summary as a function of the concepts it covers. While McDonald uses an explicit redundancy term, we model redundancy implicitly: a summary only benefits from including each concept once. With c_i an indicator for the presence of concept i in the summary, and its weight w_i, the objective function is:

$$\sum_i w_i c_i$$

We generate a summary by choosing a set of sentences that maximizes this objective function, subject to the usual length constraint.

In summing over concept weights, we assume that the value of including a concept is not effected by the presence of any other concept in the summary. That is, concepts are assumed to be independent. Choosing a suitable definition for concepts, and a mapping from the input documents to concept weights, is both important and difficult. Concepts could be words, named entities, syntactic subtrees or semantic relations, for example. While deeper semantics make more appealing concepts, their extraction and weighting are much more error-prone. Any error in concept extraction can result in a biased objective function, leading to poor sentence selection.

3 Inference by ILP

Each model presented above can be formalized as an Integer Linear Program, with a solution representing an optimal selection of sentences under the objective function, subject to a length constraint. McDonald observes that the redundancy term makes for a quadratic objective function, which he coerces to a linear function by introducing additional variables s_{ij} that represent the presence of both sentence i and sentence j in the summary. Additional constraints ensure the consistency between the sentence variables (s_i, s_j) and the quadratic term (s_{ij}). With l_i the length of sentence i and L the length limit for

[2]Strictly speaking, exact inference for the models discussed in this paper is NP-hard. Thus we use the term "scalable" in a purely practical sense.

the whole summary, the resulting ILP is:

$$\begin{aligned}
\text{Maximize: } & \sum_i Rel_i s_i - \sum_{ij} Red_{ij} s_{ij} \\
\text{Subject to: } & \sum_j l_j s_j \leq L \\
& s_{ij} \leq s_i \quad s_{ij} \leq s_j \quad \forall i, j \\
& s_i + s_j - s_{ij} \leq 1 \quad \forall i, j \\
& s_i \in \{0, 1\} \quad \forall i \\
& s_{ij} \in \{0, 1\} \quad \forall i, j
\end{aligned}$$

To express our concept-based model as an ILP, we maintain our notation from section 2, with c_i an indicator for the presence of concept i in the summary and s_j an indicator for the presence of sentence j in the summary. We add Occ_{ij} to indicate the occurrence of concept i in sentence j, resulting in a new ILP:

$$\begin{aligned}
\text{Maximize: } & \sum_i w_i c_i \\
\text{Subject to: } & \sum_j l_j s_j \leq L \\
& s_j Occ_{ij} \leq c_i, \quad \forall i, j && (1) \\
& \sum_j s_j Occ_{ij} \geq c_i \quad \forall i && (2) \\
& c_i \in \{0, 1\} \quad \forall i \\
& s_j \in \{0, 1\} \quad \forall j
\end{aligned}$$

Note that Occ, like Rel and Red, is a constant parameter. The constraints formalized in equations (1) and (2) ensure the logical consistency of the solution: selecting a sentence necessitates selecting all the concepts it contains and selecting a concept is only possible if it is present in at least one selected sentence. Constraint (1) also prevents the inclusion of concept-less sentences.

4 Performance

Here we compare both models on a common summarization task. The data is part of the Text Analysis Conference (TAC) multi-document summarization evaluation and involves generating 100-word summaries from 10 newswire documents, each on a given topic. While the 2008 edition of TAC also includes an update task—additional summaries assuming some prior knowledge—we focus only on the standard task. This includes 48 topics, averaging 235 input sentences (ranging from 47 to 652). Since the mean sentence length is around 25 words, a typical summary consists of 4 sentences.

In order to facilitate comparison, we generate summaries from both models using a common pipeline:

1. Clean input documents. A simple set of rules removes headers and formatting markup.
2. Split text into sentences. We use the unsupervised Punkt system (Kiss and Strunk, 2006).
3. Prune sentences shorter than 5 words.
4. Compute parameters needed by the models.
5. Map to ILP format and solve. We use an open source solver[3].
6. Order sentences picked by the ILP for inclusion in the summary.

The specifics of step 4 are described in detail in (McDonald, 2007) and (Gillick et al., 2008). McDonald's sentence relevance combines word-level cosine similarity with the source document and the inverse of its position (early sentences tend to be more important). Redundancy between a pair of sentences is their cosine similarity. For sentence i in document D,

$$\begin{aligned}
Rel_i &= cosine(i, D) + 1/pos(i, D) \\
Red_{ij} &= cosine(i, j)
\end{aligned}$$

In our concept-based model, we use word bigrams, weighted by the number of input documents in which they appear. While word bigrams stretch the notion of a concept a bit thin, they are easily extracted and matched (we use stemming to allow slightly more robust matching). Table 1 provides some justification for document frequency as a weighting function. Note that bigrams gave consistently better performance than unigrams or trigrams for a variety of ROUGE measures. Normalizing by document frequency measured over a generic set (TFIDF weighting) degraded ROUGE performance.

[3]gnu.org/software/glpk

Bigrams consisting of two stopwords are pruned, as are those appearing in fewer than three documents.

We largely ignore the sentence ordering problem, sorting the resulting sentences first by source document date, and then by position, so that the order of two originally adjacent sentences is preserved, for example.

Doc. Freq. (D)	1	2	3	4	5	6
In Gold Set	156	48	25	15	10	7
Not in Gold Set	5270	448	114	42	21	11
Relevant (P)	0.03	0.10	0.18	0.26	0.33	0.39

Table 1: There is a strong relationship between the document frequency of input bigrams and the fraction of those bigrams that appear in the human generated "gold" set: Let d_i be document frequency i and p_i be the percent of input bigrams with d_i that are actually in the gold set. Then the correlation $\rho(D, P) = 0.95$ for DUC 2007 and 0.97 for DUC 2006. Data here averaged over all problems in DUC 2007.

The summaries produced by the two systems have been evaluated automatically with ROUGE and manually with the Pyramid metric. In particular, ROUGE-2 is the recall in bigrams with a set of human-written abstractive summaries (Lin, 2004). The Pyramid score arises from a manual alignment of basic facts from the reference summaries, called Summary Content Units (SCUs), in a hypothesis summary (Nenkova and Passonneau, 2004). We used the SCUs provided by the TAC evaluation.

Table 2 compares these results, alongside a baseline that uses the first 100 words of the most recent document. All the scores are significantly different, showing that according to both human and automatic content evaluation, the concept-based model outperforms McDonald's sentence-based model, which in turn outperforms the baseline. Of course, the relevance and redundancy functions used for McDonald's formulation in this experiment are rather primitive, and results would likely improve with better relevance features as used in many TAC systems. Nonetheless, our system based on word bigram concepts, similarly primitive, performed at least as well as any in the TAC evaluation, according to two-tailed t-tests comparing ROUGE, Pyramid, and manually evaluated "content responsiveness" (Dang and Owczarzak, 2008) of our system and the highest scoring system in each category.

System	**ROUGE-2**	**Pyramid**
Baseline	0.058	0.186
McDonald	0.072	0.295
Concepts	0.110	0.345

Table 2: Scores for both systems and a baseline on TAC 2008 data (Set A) for ROUGE-2 and Pyramid evaluations.

5 Scalability

McDonald's sentence-level formulation corresponds to a quadratic knapsack, and he shows his particular variant is NP-hard by reduction to 3-D matching. The concept-level formulation is similar in spirit to the classical maximum coverage problem: Given a set of items X, a set of subsets S of X, and an integer k, the goal is to pick at most k subsets from S that maximizes the size of their union. Maximum coverage is known to be NP-hard by reduction to the set cover problem (Hochbaum, 1996).

Perhaps the simplest way to show that our formulation is NP-hard is by reduction to the knapsack problem (Karp, 1972). Consider the special case where sentences do not share any overlapping concepts. Then, the value of each sentence to the summary is independent of every other sentence. This is a knapsack problem: trying to maximize the value in a container of limited size. Given a solver for our problem, we could solve all knapsack problem instances, so our problem must also be NP-hard.

With n input sentences and m concepts, both formulations generate a quadratic number of constraints. However, McDonald's has $O(n^2)$ variables while ours has $O(n + m)$. In practice, scalability is largely determined by the sparsity of the redundancy matrix Red and the sentence-concept matrix Occ. Efficient solutions thus depend heavily on the choice of redundancy measure in McDonald's formulation and the choice of concepts in ours. Pruning to reduce complexity involves removing low-relevance sentences or ignoring low redundancy values in the former, and corresponds to removing low-weight concepts in the latter. Note that pruning concepts may be more desirable: Pruned sentences are irretrievable, but pruned concepts may well appear in the selected sentences through co-occurrence.

Figure 2 compares ILP run-times for the two

formulations, using a set of 25 topics from DUC 2007, each of which have at least 500 input sentences. These are very similar to the TAC 2008 topics, but more input documents are provided for each topic, which allowed us to extend the analysis to larger problems. While the ILP solver finds optimal solutions efficiently for our concept-based formulation, run-time for McDonald's approach grows very rapidly. The plot includes timing results for 250-word summaries as well, showing that our approach is fast even for much more complex problems: A rough estimate for the number of possible summaries has $\binom{500}{4} = 2.6 \times 10^9$ for 100-word summaries and $\binom{500}{10} = 2.5 \times 10^{20}$ for 250 words summaries.

While exact solutions are theoretically appealing, they are only useful in practice if fast approximations are inferior. A greedy approximation of our objective function gives 10% lower ROUGE scores than the exact solution, a gap that separates the highest scoring systems from the middle of the pack in the TAC evaluation. The greedy solution (linear in the number of sentences, assuming a constant summary length) marks an upper bound on speed and a lower bound on performance; The ILP solution marks an upper bound on performance but is subject to the perils of exponential scaling. While we have not experimented with much larger documents, approximate methods will likely be valuable in bridging the performance gap for complex problems. Preliminary experiments with local search methods are promising in this regard.

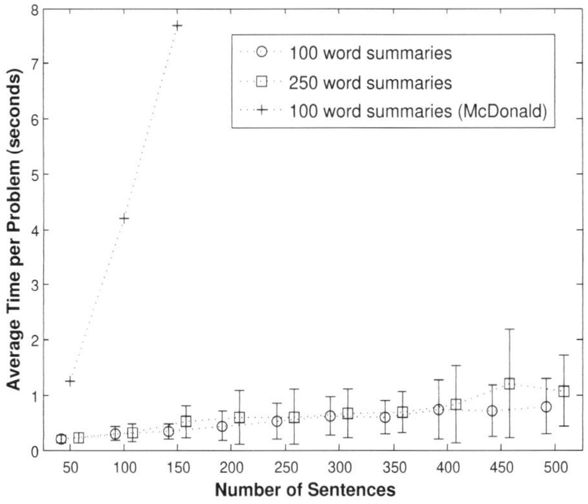

Figure 2: A comparison of ILP run-times (on an AMD 1.8Ghz desktop machine) of McDonald's sentence-based formulation and our concept-based formulation with an increasing number of input sentences.

6 Extensions

Here we describe how our ILP formulation can be extended with additional constraints to incorporate sentence compression. In particular, we are interested in creating compressed alternatives for the original sentence by manipulating its parse tree (Knight and Marcu, 2000). This idea has been applied with some success to summarization (Turner and Charniak, 2005; Hovy et al., 2005; Nenkova, 2008) with the goal of removing irrelevant or redundant details, thus freeing space for more relevant information. One way to achieve this end is to generate compressed candidates for each sentence, creating an expanded pool of input sentences, and employ some redundancy removal on the final selection (Madnani et al., 2007).

We adapt this approach to fit the ILP formulations so that the optimization procedure decides which compressed alternatives to pick. Formally, each compression candidate belongs to a group g_k corresponding to its original sentence. We can then craft a constraint to ensure that at most one sentence can be selected from group g_k, which also includes the original:

$$\sum_{i \in g_k} s_i \leq 1, \forall g_k$$

Assuming that all the compressed candidates are themselves well-formed, meaningful sentences, we would expect this approach to generate higher quality summaries. In general, however, compression algorithms can generate an exponential number of candidates. Within McDonald's framework, this can increase the number of variables and constraints tremendously. Thus, we seek a compact representation for compression in our concept framework.

Specifically, we assume that compression involves some combination of three basic operations on sentences: extraction, removal, and substitution. In extraction, a sub-sentence (perhaps the content of a quotation) may be used independently, and the rest of the sentence is dropped. In removal, a substring is dropped (a temporal clause, for example) that preserves the grammaticality of the sentence. In substitution, one substring is replaced by another (US replaces United States, for example).

Arbitrary combinations of these operations are too general to be represented efficiently in an ILP. In particular, we need to compute the length of a sentence and the concepts it covers for all compression candidates. Thus, we insist that the operations can only affect non-overlapping spans of text, and end up with a tree representation of each sentence: Nodes correspond to compression operations and leaves map to the words. Each node holds the length it contributes to the sentence recursively, as the sum of the lengths of its children. Similarly, the concepts covered by a node are the union of the concepts covered by its children. When a node is activated in the ILP, we consider that the text attached to it is present in the summary and update the length constraint and concept selection accordingly. Figure 3 gives an example of this tree representation for a sentence from the TAC data, showing the derivations of some compressed candidates.

For a given sentence j, let N_j be the set of nodes in its compression tree, $E_j \subseteq N_j$ be the set of nodes that can be extracted (used as independent sentences), $R_j \subseteq N_j$ be the set of nodes that can be removed, and $S_j \subseteq N_j$ be the set of substitution group nodes. Let x and y be nodes from N_j; we create binary variables n_x and n_y to represent the inclusion of x or y in the summary. Let $x \succ y$ denote the fact that $x \in N_j$ is a direct parent of $y \in N_j$. The constraints corresponding to the compression tree are:

$$\sum_{x \in E_j} n_x \leq 1 \quad \forall j \quad (3)$$

$$\sum_{x \succ y} n_y = n_x \quad \forall x \in S_j \quad \forall j \quad (4)$$

$$n_x \geq n_y \quad \forall (y \succ x \wedge x \notin \{R_j \cup S_j\}) \quad \forall j \quad (5)$$

$$n_x \leq n_y \quad \forall (y \succ x \wedge x \notin \{E_j \cup S_j\}) \quad \forall j \quad (6)$$

Eq. (3) enforces that only one sub-sentence is extracted from the original sentence; eq. (4) enforces that one child of a substitution group is selected if and only if the substitution node is selected; eq. (5) ensures that a child node is selected when its parent is selected unless the child is removable (or a substitution group); eq. (6) ensures that if a child node is selected, its parent is also selected unless the child is an extraction node (that can be used as a root).

Each node is associated with the words and the concepts it contains directly (which are not contained by a child node) in order to compute the new length constraints and activate concepts in the objective function. We set Occ_{ix} to represent the occurrence of concept i in node x as a direct child. Let l_x be the length contributed to node x as direct children. The resulting ILP for performing sentence compression jointly with sentence selection is:

$$\begin{aligned} \text{Maximize: } & \sum_i w_i c_i \\ \text{Subject to: } & \sum_j l_x n_x \leq L \\ & n_x Occ_{ix} \leq c_i, \quad \forall i, x \\ & \sum_x n_x Occ_{ix} \geq c_i \quad \forall i \\ & \text{idem constraints (3) to (6)} \\ & c_i \in \{0, 1\} \quad \forall i \\ & n_x \in \{0, 1\} \quad \forall x \end{aligned}$$

While this framework can be used to implement a wide range of compression techniques, we choose to derive the compression tree from the sentence's parse tree, extracted with the Berkeley parser (Petrov and Klein, 2007), and use a set of rules to label parse tree nodes with compression operations. For example, declarative clauses containing a subject and a verb are labeled with the extract (E) operation; adverbial clauses and non-mandatory prepositional clauses are labeled with the remove (R) operation; Acronyms can be replaced by their full form by using substitution (S) operations and a primitive form of co-reference resolution is used to allow the substitution of noun phrases by their referent.

System	**R-2**	**Pyr.**	**LQ**
No comp.	0.110	0.345	2.479
Comp.	0.111	0.323	2.021

Table 3: Scores of the system with and without sentence compression included in the ILP (TAC'08 Set A data).

When implemented in the system presented in section 4, this approach gives a slight improvement

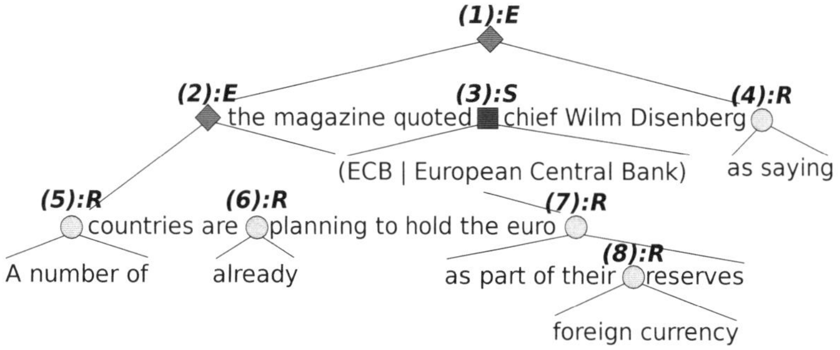

Node	**Len.**	**Concepts**
(1):E	6	{the_magazine, magazine_quoted, chief_Wilm, Wilm_Disenberg}
(2):E	7	{countries_are, planning_to, to_hold, hold_the, the_euro}
(3):S	0	{}
(3a)	1	{ECB}
(3b)	3	{European_Central, Central_Bank}
(4):R	2	{as_saying}
(5):R	3	{a_number, number_of}
(6):R	1	{}
(7):R	5	{as_part, part_of, reserves}
(8):R	2	{foreign_currency}

- Original: *A number of Countries are already planning to hold the euro as part of their foreign currency reserves, the magazine quoted European Central Bank chief Wim Duisenberg as saying.*
- [1,2,5,3a]: *A number of countries are planning to hold the euro, the magazine quoted ECB chief Wim Duisenberg.*
- [2,5,6,7,8]: *A number of countries are already planning to hold the euro as part of their foreign currency reserves.*
- [2,7,8]: *Countries are planning to hold the euro as part of their foreign currency reserves.*
- [2]: *Countries are planning to hold the euro.*

Figure 3: A compression tree for an example sentence. E-nodes (diamonds) can be extracted and used as an independent sentences, R-nodes (circles) can be removed, and S-nodes (squares) contain substitution alternatives. The table shows the word bigram concepts covered by each node and the length it contributes to the summary. Examples of resulting compression candidates are given on the right side, with the list of nodes activated in their derivations.

in ROUGE-2 score (see Table 3), but a reduction in Pyramid score. An analysis of the resulting summaries showed that the rules used for implementing sentence compression fail to ensure that all compression candidates are valid sentences, and about 60% of the summaries contain ungrammatical sentences. This is confirmed by the linguistic quality[4] score drop for this system. The poor quality of the compressed sentences explains the reduction in Pyramid scores: Human judges tend to not give credit to ungrammatical sentences because they obscure the SCUs.

We have shown in this section how sentence compression can be implemented in a more scalable way under the concept-based model, but it remains to be shown that such a technique can improve summary quality.

7 Related work

In addition to proposing an ILP for the sentence-level model, McDonald (2007) discusses a kind of summary-level model: The score of a summary is determined by its cosine similarity to the collection of input documents. Though this idea is only implemented with approximate methods, it is similar in spirit to our concept-based model since it relies on weights for individual summary words rather than sentences.

Using a maximum coverage model for summarization is not new. Filatova (2004) formalizes the idea, discussing its similarity to the classical NP-hard problem, but in the end uses a greedy approximation to generate summaries. More recently, Yih et al. (2007) employ a similar model and uses a stack decoder to improve on a greedy search. Globally optimal summaries are also discussed by Liu (2006) and Jaoua Kallel (2004) who apply genetic algorithms for finding selections of sentences that maximize summary-level metrics. Hassel (2006) uses hill climbing to build summaries that maximize a global information criterion based on random indexing.

The general idea of concept-level scoring for summarization is employed in the SumBasic system (Nenkova and Vanderwende, 2005), which chooses sentences greedily according to the sum of their word values (values are derived from fre-

[4]As measured according to the TAC'08 guidelines.

quency). Conroy (2006) describes a bag-of-words model, with the goal of approximating the distribution of words from the input documents in the summary. Others, like (Yih et al., 2007) train a model to learn the value of each word from a set of features including frequency and position. Filatova's model is most theoretically similar to ours, though the concepts she chooses are "events".

8 Conclusion and Future Work

We have synthesized a number of ideas from the field of automatic summarization, including concept-level weighting, a maximum coverage model to minimize redundancy globally, and sentence compression derived from parse trees. While an ILP formulation for summarization is not novel, ours provides reasonably scalable, efficient solutions for practical problems, including those in recent TAC and DUC evaluations. We have also shown how it can be extended to perform sentence compression and sentence selection jointly.

In ROUGE and Pyramid evaluation, our system significantly outperformed McDonald's ILP system. However, we would note that better design of sentence-level scoring would likely yield better results as suggested by the success of greedy sentence-based methods at the DUC and TAC conferences (see for instance (Toutanova et al., 2007)). Still, the performance of our system, on par with the current state-of-the-art, is encouraging.

There are three principal directions for future work. First, word bigram concepts are convenient, but semantically unappealing. We plan to explore concepts derived from parse trees, where weights may be a function of frequency as well as hierarchical relationships.

Second, our current approach relies entirely on word frequency, a reasonable proxy for relevance, but likely inferior to learning weights from training data. A number of systems have shown improvements by learning word values, though preliminary attempts to improve on our frequency heuristic by learning bigram values have not produced significant gains. Better features may be necessary. However, since the ILP gives optimal solutions so quickly, we are more interested in discriminative training where we learn weights for features that push the resulting summaries in the right direction, as opposed to the individual concept values.

Third, our rule-based sentence compression is more of a proof of concept, showing that joint compression and optimal selection is feasible. Better statistical methods have been developed for producing high quality compression candidates (McDonald, 2006), that maintain linguistic quality, some recent work even uses ILPs for exact inference (Clarke and Lapata, 2008). The addition of compressed sentences tends to yield less coherent summaries, making sentence ordering more important. We would like to add constraints on sentence ordering to the ILP formulation to address this issue.

Acknowledgments

This work is supported by the Defense Advanced Research Projects Agency (DARPA) GALE project, under Contract No. HR0011-06-C-0023. Any opinions, findings, conclusions or recommendations expressed in this material are those of the authors and do not necessarily reflect the views of DARPA.

References

James Clarke and Mirella Lapata. 2008. Global inference for sentence compression: An integer linear programming approach. *Journal of Artificial Intelligence Research*, 31:273–381.

John M. Conroy, Judith D. Schlesinger, and Dianne P. O'Leary. 2006. Topic-focused multi-document summarization using an approximate oracle score. In *Proceedings of COLING/ACL*.

Hoa Trang Dang and Karolina Owczarzak. 2008. Overview of the TAC 2008 Update Summarization Task. In *Proceedings of Text Analysis Conference*.

E. Filatova and V. Hatzivassiloglou. 2004. Event-based extractive summarization. In *Proceedings of ACL Workshop on Summarization*, volume 111.

G. Gallo, PL Hammer, and B. Simeone. 1980. Quadratic knapsack problems. *Mathematical Programming Study*, 12:132–149.

D. Gillick, B. Favre, and D. Hakkani-Tur. 2008. The ICSI Summarization System at TAC 2008. In *Proceedings of the Text Understanding Conference*.

Jade Goldstein, Vibhu Mittal, Jaime Carbonell, and Mark Kantrowitz. 2000. Multi-document summarization by sentence extraction. *Proceedings of the ANLP/NAACL Workshop on Automatic Summarization*, pages 40–48.

Martin Hassel and Jonas Sjöbergh. 2006. Towards holistic summarization: Selecting summaries, not sentences. In *Proceedings of Language Resources and Evaluation*.

D.S. Hochbaum. 1996. Approximating covering and packing problems: set cover, vertex cover, independent set, and related problems. *PWS Publishing Co. Boston, MA, USA*, pages 94–143.

E. Hovy, C.Y. Lin, and L. Zhou. 2005. A BE-based multi-document summarizer with sentence compression. In *Proceedings of Multilingual Summarization Evaluation*.

Fatma Jaoua Kallel, Maher Jaoua, Lamia Belguith Hadrich, and Abdelmajid Ben Hamadou. 2004. Summarization at LARIS Laboratory. In *Proceedings of the Document Understanding Conference*.

Richard Manning Karp. 1972. Reducibility among combinatorial problems. *Complexity of Computer Computations*, 43:85–103.

Tibor Kiss and Jan Strunk. 2006. Unsupervised multilingual sentence boundary detection. *Computational Linguistics*, 32.

K. Knight and D. Marcu. 2000. Statistics-Based Summarization-Step One: Sentence Compression. In *Proceedings of the National Conference on Artificial Intelligence*, pages 703–710. Menlo Park, CA; Cambridge, MA; London; AAAI Press; MIT Press; 1999.

Chin-Yew Lin. 2004. ROUGE: A Package for Automatic Evaluation of Summaries. In *Proceedings of the Workshop on Text Summarization Branches Out (WAS 2004)*, pages 25–26.

D. Liu, Y. Wang, C. Liu, and Z. Wang. 2006. Multiple Documents Summarization Based on Genetic Algorithm. *Lecture Notes in Computer Science*, 4223:355.

N. Madnani, D. Zajic, B. Dorr, N.F. Ayan, and J. Lin. 2007. Multiple Alternative Sentence Compressions for Automatic Text Summarization. In *Proceedings of the Document Understanding Conference at NLT/NAACL*.

R. McDonald. 2006. Discriminative sentence compression with soft syntactic constraints. In *Proceedings of the 11th EACL*, pages 297–304.

R. McDonald. 2007. A Study of Global Inference Algorithms in Multi-document Summarization. *Lecture Notes in Computer Science*, 4425:557.

Ani Nenkova and Rebecca Passonneau. 2004. Evaluating content selection in summarization: The pyramid method. In *Proceedings of HLT-NAACL*.

A. Nenkova and L. Vanderwende. 2005. The impact of frequency on summarization. Technical Report MSR-TR-2005-101, Microsoft Research, Redmond, Washington.

A. Nenkova. 2008. Entity-driven rewrite for multidocument summarization. *Proceedings of IJCNLP*.

Slav Petrov and Dan Klein. 2007. Learning and inference for hierarchically split PCFGs. In *AAAI 2007 (Nectar Track)*.

D. Pisinger, A.B. Rasmussen, and R. Sandvik. 2005. Solution of large-sized quadratic knapsack problems through aggressive reduction. *INFORMS Journal on Computing*.

K. Toutanova, C. Brockett, M. Gamon, J. Jagarlamudi, H. Suzuki, and L. Vanderwende. 2007. The Pythy Summarization System: Microsoft Research at DUC 2007. In *Proceedings of the Document Understanding Conference*.

J. Turner and E. Charniak. 2005. Supervised and Unsupervised Learning for Sentence Compression. In *Proceedings of ACL*.

W. Yih, J. Goodman, L. Vanderwende, and H. Suzuki. 2007. Multi-document summarization by maximizing informative content-words. In *International Joint Conference on Artificial Intelligence*.

Bounding and Comparing Methods for Correlation Clustering Beyond ILP

Micha Elsner and Warren Schudy
Department of Computer Science
Brown University
Providence, RI 02912
{melsner,ws}@cs.brown.edu

Abstract

We evaluate several heuristic solvers for correlation clustering, the NP-hard problem of partitioning a dataset given pairwise affinities between all points. We experiment on two practical tasks, document clustering and chat disentanglement, to which ILP does not scale. On these datasets, we show that the clustering objective often, but not always, correlates with external metrics, and that local search always improves over greedy solutions. We use semi-definite programming (SDP) to provide a tighter bound, showing that simple algorithms are already close to optimality.

1 Introduction

Correlation clustering is a powerful technique for discovering structure in data. It operates on the pairwise relationships between datapoints, partitioning the graph to minimize the number of unrelated pairs that are clustered together, plus the number of related pairs that are separated. Unfortunately, this minimization problem is NP-hard (Ailon et al., 2008). Practical work has adopted one of three strategies for solving it. For a few specific tasks, one can restrict the problem so that it is efficiently solvable. In most cases, however, this is impossible. Integer linear programming (ILP) can be used to solve the general problem optimally, but only when the number of data points is small. Beyond a few hundred points, the only available solutions are heuristic or approximate.

In this paper, we evaluate a variety of solutions for correlation clustering on two realistic NLP tasks, text topic clustering and chat disentanglement, where typical datasets are too large for ILP to find a solution. We show, as in previous work on consensus clustering (Goder and Filkov, 2008), that local search can improve the solutions found by commonly-used methods. We investigate the relationship between the clustering objective and external evaluation metrics such as F-score and one-to-one overlap, showing that optimizing the objective is usually a reasonable aim, but that other measurements like number of clusters found should sometimes be used to reject pathological solutions. We prove that the best heuristics are quite close to optimal, using the first implementation of the semi-definite programming (SDP) relaxation to provide tighter bounds.

The specific algorithms we investigate are, of course, only a subset of the large number of possible solutions, or even of those proposed in the literature. We chose to test a few common, efficient algorithms that are easily implemented. Our use of a good bounding strategy means that we do not need to perform an exhaustive comparison; we will show that, though the methods we describe are not perfect, the remaining improvements possible with any algorithm are relatively small.

2 Previous Work

Correlation clustering was first introduced by Ben-Dor et al. (1999) to cluster gene expression patterns. The correlation clustering approach has several strengths. It does not require users to specify a parametric form for the clusters, nor to pick the number of clusters. Unlike fully unsupervised clus-

Proceedings of the NAACL HLT Workshop on Integer Linear Programming for Natural Language Processing, pages 19–27,
Boulder, Colorado, June 2009.

tering methods, it can use training data to optimize the pairwise classifier, but unlike classification, it does not require samples from the specific clusters found in the test data. For instance, it can use messages about cars to learn a similarity function that can then be applied to messages about atheism.

Correlation clustering is a standard method for coreference resolution. It was introduced to the area by Soon et al. (2001), who describe the first-link heuristic method for solving it. Ng and Cardie (2002) extend this work with better features, and develop the best-link heuristic, which finds better solutions. McCallum and Wellner (2004) explicitly describe the problem as correlation clustering and use an approximate technique (Bansal et al., 2004) to enforce transitivity. Recently Finkel and Manning (2008) show that the optimal ILP solution outperforms the first and best-link methods. Cohen and Richman (2002) experiment with various heuristic solutions for the cross-document coreference task of grouping references to named entities.

Finally, correlation clustering has proven useful in several discourse tasks. Barzilay and Lapata (2006) use it for content aggregation in a generation system. In Malioutov and Barzilay (2006), it is used for topic segmentation—since segments must be contiguous, the problem can be solved in polynomial time. Elsner and Charniak (2008) address the related problem of disentanglement (which we explore in Section 5.3), doing inference with the voting greedy algorithm.

Bertolacci and Wirth (2007), Goder and Filkov (2008) and Gionis et al. (2007) conduct experiments on the closely related problem of *consensus clustering*, often solved by reduction to correlation clustering. The input to this problem is a set of clusterings; the output is a "median" clustering which minimizes the sum of (Rand) distance to the inputs. Although these papers investigate some of the same algorithms we use, they use an unrealistic lower bound, and so cannot convincingly evaluate absolute performance. Gionis et al. (2007) give an external evaluation on some UCI datasets, but this is somewhat unconvincing since their metric, the *impurity index*, which is essentially precision ignoring recall, gives a perfect score to the all-singletons clustering. The other two papers are based on objective values, not external metrics.[1]

A variety of approximation algorithms for correlation clustering with worst-case theoretical guarantees have been proposed: (Bansal et al., 2004; Ailon et al., 2008; Demaine et al., 2006; Charikar et al., 2005; Giotis and Guruswami, 2006). Researchers including (Ben-Dor et al., 1999; Joachims and Hopcroft, 2005; Mathieu and Schudy, 2008) study correlation clustering theoretically when the input is generated by randomly perturbing an unknown ground truth clustering.

3 Algorithms

We begin with some notation and a formal definition of the problem. Our input is a complete, undirected graph G with n nodes; each edge in the graph has a probability p_{ij} reflecting our belief as to whether nodes i and j come from the same cluster. Our goal is to find a clustering, defined as a new graph G' with edges $x_{ij} \in \{0, 1\}$, where if $x_{ij} = 1$, nodes i and j are assigned to the same cluster. To make this consistent, the edges must define an equivalence relationship: $x_{ii} = 1$ and $x_{ij} = x_{jk} = 1$ implies $x_{ij} = x_{ik}$.

Our objective is to find a clustering as consistent as possible with our beliefs—edges with high probability should not cross cluster boundaries, and edges with low probability should. We define w_{ij}^+ as the cost of cutting an edge whose probability is p_{ij} and w_{ij}^- as the cost of keeping it. Mathematically, this objective can be written (Ailon et al., 2008; Finkel and Manning, 2008) as:

$$\min \sum_{ij:i<j} x_{ij} w_{ij}^- + (1 - x_{ij}) w_{ij}^+. \qquad (1)$$

There are two plausible definitions for the costs w^+ and w^-, both of which have gained some support in the literature. We can take $w_{ij}^+ = p_{ij}$ and $w_{ij}^- = 1 - p_{ij}$ (*additive* weights) as in (Ailon et al., 2008) and others, or $w_{ij}^+ = \log(p_{ij}), w_{ij}^- = \log(1 - p_{ij})$ (*logarithmic* weights) as in (Finkel and Manning, 2008). The logarithmic scheme has a tenuous mathematical justification, since it selects a maximum-likelihood clustering under the assumption that the

[1] Bertolacci and Wirth (2007) gave normalized mutual information for one algorithm and data set, but almost all of their results study objective value only.

p_{ij} are independent and identically distributed given the status of the edge ij in the true clustering. If we obtain the p_{ij} using a classifier, however, this assumption is obviously untrue—some nodes will be easy to link, while others will be hard—so we evaluate the different weighting schemes empirically.

3.1 Greedy Methods

We use four greedy methods drawn from the literature; they are both fast and easy to implement. All of them make decisions based on the *net weight* $w^{\pm}_{ij} = w^{+}_{ij} - w^{-}_{ij}$.

These algorithms step through the nodes of the graph according to a permutation π. We try 100 random permutations for each algorithm and report the run which attains the best objective value (typically this is slightly better than the average run; we discuss this more in the experimental sections). To simplify the pseudocode we label the vertices $1, 2, \ldots n$ in the order specified by π. After this relabeling $\pi(i) = i$ so π need not appear explicitly in the algorithms.

Three of the algorithms are given in Figure 1. All three algorithms start with the empty clustering and add the vertices one by one. The BEST algorithm adds each vertex i to the cluster with the strongest $w^{\pm}$ connecting to i, or to a new singleton if none of the $w^{\pm}$ are positive. The FIRST algorithm adds each vertex i to the cluster containing the most recently considered vertex j with $w^{\pm}_{ij} > 0$. The VOTE algorithm adds each vertex to the cluster that minimizes the correlation clustering objective, i.e. to the cluster maximizing the total net weight or to a singleton if no total is positive.

Ailon et al. (2008) introduced the PIVOT algorithm, given in Figure 2, and proved that it is a 5-approximation if $w^{+}_{ij} + w^{-}_{ij} = 1$ for all i, j and π is chosen randomly. Unlike BEST, VOTE and FIRST, which build clusters vertex by vertex, the PIVOT algorithm creates each new cluster in its final form. This algorithm repeatedly takes an unclustered pivot vertex and creates a new cluster containing that vertex and all unclustered neighbors with positive weight.

3.2 Local Search

We use the straightforward local search previously used by Gionis et al. (2007) and Goder and Filkov

$k \leftarrow 0$ // number of clusters created so far
for $i = 1 \ldots n$ **do**
  for $c = 1 \ldots k$ **do**
    if BEST **then**
      $Quality_c \leftarrow \max_{j \in C[c]} w^{\pm}_{ij}$
    else if FIRST **then**
      $Quality_c \leftarrow \max_{j \in C[c] : w^{\pm}_{ij} > 0} j$
    else if VOTE **then**
      $Quality_c \leftarrow \sum_{j \in C[c]} w^{\pm}_{ij}$
  $c^* \leftarrow \arg\max_{1 \le c \le k} Quality_c$
  if $Quality_{c^*} > 0$ **then**
    $C[c^*] \leftarrow C[c^*] \cup \{i\}$
  else
    $C[k{+}{+}] \leftarrow \{i\}$ // form a new cluster

Figure 1: BEST/FIRST/VOTE algorithms

$k \leftarrow 0$ // number of clusters created so far
for $i = 1 \ldots n$ **do**
  $P \leftarrow \bigcup_{1 \le c \le k} C[c]$ // Vertices already placed
  if $i \notin P$ **then**
    $C[k{+}{+}] \leftarrow \{i\} \cup \{i < j \le n : j \notin P \text{ and } w^{\pm}_{ij} > 0\}$

Figure 2: PIVOT algorithm by Ailon et al. (2008)

(2008). The allowed *one element moves* consist of removing one vertex from a cluster and either moving it to another cluster or to a new singleton cluster. The best one element move (BOEM) algorithm repeatedly makes the most profitable best one element move until a local optimum is reached. *Simulated Annealing* (SA) makes a random single-element move, with probability related to the difference in objective it causes and the current temperature. Our annealing schedule is exponential and designed to attempt $2000n$ moves for n nodes. We initialize the local search either with all nodes clustered together, or at the clustering produced by one of our greedy algorithms (in our tables, the latter is written, eg. PIVOT/BOEM, if the greedy algorithm is PIVOT).

4 Bounding with SDP

Although comparing different algorithms to one another gives a good picture of relative performance, it is natural to wonder how well they do in an absolute sense—how they compare to the optimal solution.

For very small instances, we can actually find the optimum using ILP, but since this does not scale beyond a few hundred points (see Section 5.1), for realistic instances we must instead bound the optimal value. Bounds are usually obtained by solving a *relaxation* of the original problem: a simpler problem with the same objective but fewer constraints.

The bound used in previous work (Goder and Filkov, 2008; Gionis et al., 2007; Bertolacci and Wirth, 2007), which we call the *trivial bound*, is obtained by ignoring the transitivity constraints entirely. To optimize, we link ($x_{ij} = 1$) all the pairs where w^+_{ij} is larger than w^-_{ij}; since this solution is quite far from being a clustering, the bound tends not to be very tight.

To get a better idea of how good a real clustering can be, we use a semi-definite programming (SDP) relaxation to provide a better bound. Here we motivate and define this relaxation.

One can picture a clustering geometrically by associating cluster c with the standard basis vector $e_c = (\underbrace{0,0,\ldots,0}_{c-1},1,\underbrace{0,\ldots,0}_{n-c}) \in \mathbb{R}^n$. If object i is in cluster c then it is natural to associate i with the vector $r_i = e_c$. This gives a nice geometric picture of a clustering, with objects i and j in the same cluster if and only if $r_i = r_j$. Note that the dot product $r_i \bullet r_j$ is 1 if i and j are in the same cluster and 0 otherwise. These ideas yield a simple reformulation of the correlation clustering problem:

$$\begin{array}{c}\min_r \sum_{i,j:i<j} (r_i \bullet r_j) w^-_{ij} + (1 - r_j \bullet r_j) w^+_{ij} \\ \text{s.t. } \forall i \ \ \exists c : r_i = e_c\end{array}$$

To get an efficiently computable lower-bound we relax the constraints that the r_is are standard basis vectors, replacing them with two sets of constraints: $r_i \bullet r_i = 1$ for all i and $r_i \bullet r_j \geq 0$ for all i, j.

Since the r_i only appear as dot products, we can rewrite in terms of $x_{ij} = r_i \bullet r_j$. However, we must now constrain the x_{ij} to be the dot products of some set of vectors in $\mathbb{R}^n$. This is true if and only if the symmetric matrix $X = \{x_{ij}\}_{ij}$ is *positive semi-definite*. We now have the standard semi-definite programming (SDP) relaxation of correlation clustering (e.g. (Charikar et al., 2005; Mathieu and Schudy, 2008)):

$$\begin{array}{l}\min_x \sum_{i,j:i<j} x_{ij} w^-_{ij} + (1 - x_{ij}) w^+_{ij} \\ \text{s.t.} \begin{cases} x_{ii} = 1 & \forall i \\ x_{ij} \geq 0 & \forall i,j \\ X = \{x_{ij}\}_{ij} \text{ PSD} & \end{cases} .\end{array}$$

This SDP has been studied theoretically by a number of authors; we mention just two here. Charikar et al. (2005) give an approximation algorithm based on rounding the SDP which is a 0.7664 approximation for the problem of maximizing agreements. Mathieu and Schudy (2008) show that if the input is generated by corrupting the edges of a ground truth clustering B independently, then the SDP relaxation value is within an additive $O(n\sqrt{n})$ of the optimum clustering. They further show that using the PIVOT algorithm to round the SDP yields a clustering with value at most $O(n\sqrt{n})$ more than optimal.

5 Experiments

5.1 Scalability

Using synthetic data, we investigate the scalability of the linear programming solver and SDP bound. To find optimal solutions, we pass the complete ILP[2] to CPLEX. This is reasonable for 100 points and solvable for 200; beyond this point it cannot be solved due to memory exhaustion. As noted below, despite our inability to compute the LP bound on large instances, we can sometimes prove that they must be worse than SDP bounds, so we do not investigate LP-solving techniques further.

The SDP has fewer constraints than the ILP ($O(n^2)$ vs $O(n^3)$), but this is still more than many SDP solvers can handle. For our experiments we used one of the few SDP solvers that can handle such a large number of constraints: Christoph Helmberg's ConicBundle library (Helmberg, 2009; Helmberg, 2000). This solver can handle several thousand datapoints. It produces loose lower-bounds (off by a few percent) quickly but converges to optimality quite slowly; we err on the side of inefficiency by running for up to 60 hours. Of course, the SDP solver is only necessary to bound algorithm performance; our solvers themselves scale much better.

[2]Consisting of the objective plus constraints $0 \leq x_{ij} \leq 1$ and triangle inequality (Ailon et al., 2008).

5.2 Twenty Newsgroups

In this section, we test our approach on a typical benchmark clustering dataset, 20 Newsgroups, which contains posts from a variety of Usenet newsgroups such as `rec.motorcycles` and `alt.atheism`. Since our bounding technique does not scale to the full dataset, we restrict our attention to a subsample of 100 messages[3] from each newsgroup for a total of 2000—still a realistically large-scale problem. Our goal is to cluster messages by their newsgroup of origin. We conduct experiments by holding out four newsgroups as a training set, learning a pairwise classifier, and applying it to the remaining 16 newsgroups to form our affinity matrix.[4]

Our pairwise classifier uses three types of features previously found useful in document clustering. First, we bucket all words[5] by their log document frequency (for an overview of TF-IDF see (Joachims, 1997)). For a pair of messages, we create a feature for each bucket whose value is the proportion of shared words in that bucket. Secondly, we run LSA (Deerwester et al., 1990) on the TF-IDF matrix for the dataset, and use the cosine distance between each message pair as a feature. Finally, we use the same type of shared words features for terms in message subjects. We make a training instance for each pair of documents in the training set and learn via logistic regression.

The classifier has an average F-score of 29% and an accuracy of 88%—not particularly good. We should emphasize that the clustering task for 20 newsgroups is much harder than the more common classification task—since our training set is entirely disjoint with the testing set, we can only learn weights on feature categories, not term weights. Our aim is to create realistic-looking data on which to test our clustering methods, not to motivate correlation clustering as a solution to this specific problem. In fact, Zhong and Ghosh (2003) report better results using generative models.

We evaluate our clusterings using three different metrics (see Meila (2007) for an overview of clustering metrics). The *Rand* measure counts the number of pairs of points for which the proposed clustering agrees with ground truth. This is the metric which is mathematically closest to the objective. However, since most points are in different clusters, any solution with small clusters tends to get a high score. Therefore we also report the more sensitive *F-score* with respect to the minority ("same cluster") class. We also report the *one-to-one* score, which measures accuracy over single points. For this metric, we calculate a maximum-weight matching between proposed clusters and ground-truth clusters, then report the overlap between the two.

When presenting objective values, we locate them within the range between the trivial lower bound dis-

Logarithmic Weights

	Obj	Rand	F	1-1
SDP bound	51.1%	-	-	-
VOTE/BOEM	55.8%	93.80	33	41
SA	56.3%	93.56	31	36
PIVOT/BOEM	56.6%	93.63	32	39
BEST/BOEM	57.6%	93.57	31	38
FIRST/BOEM	57.9%	93.65	30	36
VOTE	59.0%	93.41	29	35
BOEM	60.1%	93.51	30	35
PIVOT	100%	90.85	17	27
BEST	138%	87.11	20	29
FIRST	619%	40.97	11	8

Additive Weights

	Obj	Rand	F	1-1
SDP bound	59.0%	-	-	-
SA	63.5%	93.75	32	39
VOTE/BOEM	63.5%	93.75	32	39
PIVOT/BOEM	63.7%	93.70	32	39
BEST/BOEM	63.8%	93.73	31	39
FIRST/BOEM	63.9%	93.58	31	37
BOEM	64.6%	93.65	31	37
VOTE	67.3%	93.35	28	34
PIVOT	109%	90.63	17	26
BEST	165%	87.06	20	29
FIRST	761%	40.46	11	8

Table 1: Score of the solution with best objective for each solver, averaged over newsgroups training sets, sorted by objective.

[3]Available as `mini_newsgroups.tar.gz` from the UCI machine learning repository.

[4]The experiments below are averaged over four disjoint training sets.

[5]We omit the message header, except the subject line, and also discard word types with fewer than 3 occurrences.

cussed in Section 4 and the objective value of the singletons clustering ($x_{ij} = 0, i \neq j$). On this scale, lower is better; 0% corresponds to the trivial bound and 100% corresponds to the singletons clustering. It is possible to find values greater than 100%, since some particularly bad clusterings have objectives worse than the singletons clustering. Plainly, however, real clusterings will not have values as low as 0%, since the trivial bound is so unrealistic.

Our results are shown in Table 1. The best results are obtained using logarithmic weights with VOTE followed by BOEM; reasonable results are also found using additive weights, and annealing, VOTE or PIVOT followed by BOEM. On its own, the best greedy scheme is VOTE, but all of them are substantially improved by BOEM. First-link is by far the worst. Our use of the SDP lower bound rather than the trivial lower-bound of 0% reduces the gap between the best clustering and the lower bound by over a factor of ten. It is easy to show that the LP relaxation can obtain a bound of at most 50%[6]—the SDP beats the LP in both runtime and quality!

We analyze the correlation between objective values and metric values, averaging Kendall's tau[7] over the four datasets (Table 2). Over the entire dataset, correlations are generally good (large and negative), showing that optimizing the objective is indeed a useful way to find good results. We also examine correlations for the solutions with objective values within the top 10%. Here the correlation is much poorer; selecting the solution with the best objective value will not necessarily optimize the metric, although the correspondence is slightly better for the log-weights scheme. The correlations do exist, however, and so the solution with the best objective value is typically slightly better than the median.

In Figure 3, we show the distribution of one-to-one scores obtained (for one specific dataset) by the best solvers. From this diagram, it is clear that log-weights and VOTE/BOEM usually obtain the best scores for this metric, since the median is higher than other solvers' upper quartile scores. All solvers have quite high variance, with a range of about 2% between quartiles and 4% overall. We omit the F-score plot, which is similar, for space reasons.

[6]The solution $x_{ij} = \frac{1}{2}\mathbb{1}\left(w_{ij}^{-} > w_{ij}^{+}\right)$ for $i < j$ is feasible in the LP.

[7]The standard Pearson correlation coefficient is less robust to outliers, which causes problems for this data.

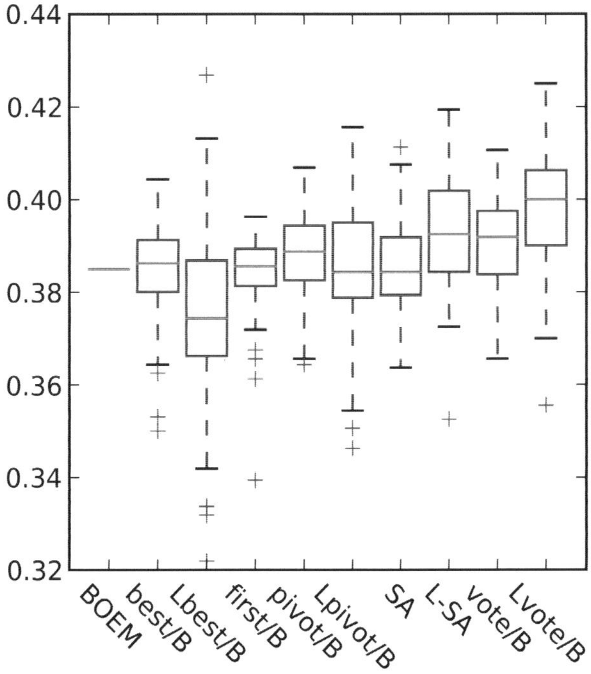

Figure 3: Box-and-whisker diagram (outliers as +) for one-to-one scores obtained by the best few solvers on a particular newsgroup dataset. L means using log weights. B means improved with BOEM.

	Rand	F	1-1
Log-wt	-.60	-.73	-.71
Top 10 %	-.14	-.22	-.24
Add-wt	-.60	-.67	-.65
Top 10 %	-.13	-.15	-.14

Table 2: Kendall's tau correlation between objective and metric values, averaged over newsgroup datasets, for all solutions and top 10% of solutions.

5.3 Chat Disentanglement

In the disentanglement task, we examine data from a shared discussion group where many conversations are occurring simultaneously. The task is to partition the utterances into a set of conversations. This task differs from newsgroup clustering in that data points (utterances) have an inherent linear order. Ordering is typical in discourse tasks including topic segmentation and coreference resolution.

We use the annotated dataset and pairwise classifier made available by Elsner and Charniak (2008);[8] this study represents a competitive baseline, although more recently Wang and Oard (2009) have improved it. Since this classifier is ineffective at linking utterances more than 129 seconds apart, we treat all decisions for such utterances as abstentions, $p = .5$. For utterance pairs on which it does make a decision, the classifier has a reported accuracy of 75% with an F-score of 71%.

As in previous work, we run experiments on the 800-utterance test set and average metrics over 6 test annotations. We evaluate using the three metrics reported by previous work. Two node-counting metrics measure global accuracy: *one-to-one match* as explained above, and *Shen's F* (Shen et al., 2006): $F = \sum_i \frac{n_i}{n} \max_j(F(i,j))$. Here i is a gold conversation with size n_i and j is a proposed conversation with size n_j, sharing n_{ij} utterances; $F(i,j)$ is the harmonic mean of precision ($\frac{n_{ij}}{n_j}$) and recall ($\frac{n_{ij}}{n_i}$). A third metric, the *local agreement*, counts edgewise agreement for pairs of nearby utterances, where nearby means "within three utterances."

In this dataset, the SDP is a more moderate improvement over the trivial lower bound, reducing the gap between the best clustering and best lower bound by a factor of about 3 (Table 3).

Optimization of the objective does not correspond to improvements in the global metrics (Table 3); for instance, the best objectives are attained with FIRST/BOEM, but VOTE/BOEM yields better one-to-one and F scores. Correlation between the objective and these global metrics is extremely weak (Table 5). The local metric is somewhat correlated.

Local search does improve metric results for each particular greedy algorithm. For instance, when BOEM is added to VOTE (with log weights), one-to-one increases from 44% to 46%, local from 72% to 73% and F from 48% to 50%. This represents a moderate improvement on the inference scheme described in Elsner and Charniak (2008). They use voting with additive weights, but rather than performing multiple runs over random permutations, they process utterances in the order they occur. (We experimented with processing in order; the results are unclear, but there is a slight trend toward worse performance, as in this case.) Their results (also shown in the table) are 41% one-to-one, 73% local and .44% F-score.[9] Our improvement on the global metrics (12% relative improvement in one-to-one, 13% in F-score) is modest, but was achieved with better inference on exactly the same input.

Since the objective function fails to distinguish good solutions from bad ones, we examine the types of solutions found by different methods in the hope of explaining why some perform better than others. In this setting, some methods (notably local search run on its own or from a poor starting point) find far fewer clusters than others (Table 4; log weights not shown but similar to additive). Since the classifier abstains for utterances more than 129 seconds apart, the objective is unaffected if very distant utterances are linked on the basis of little or no evidence; this is presumably how such large clusters form. (This raises the question of whether abstentions should be given weaker links with $p < .5$. We leave this for future work.) Algorithms which find reasonable numbers of clusters (VOTE, PIVOT, BEST and local searches based on these) all achieve good metric scores, although there is still no reliable way to find the best solution among this set of methods.

6 Conclusions

It is clear from these results that heuristic methods can provide good correlation clustering solutions on datasets far too large for ILP to scale. The particular solver chosen[10] has a substantial impact on the quality of results obtained, in terms of external metrics as well as objective value.

For general problems, our recommendation is to use log weights and run VOTE/BOEM. This algorithm is fast, achieves good objective values, and yields good metric scores on our datasets. Although objective values are usually only weakly correlated with metrics, our results suggest that slightly better scores can be obtained by running the algorithm many times and returning the solution with the best objective. This may be worth trying even when the datapoints are inherently ordered, as in chat.

[8] Downloaded from cs.brown.edu/~melsner

[9] The F-score metric is not used in Elsner and Charniak (2008); we compute it ourselves on the result produced by their software.

[10] Our C++ correlation clustering software and SDP bounding package are available for download from cs.brown.edu/~melsner.

Log Weights				
	Obj	1-1	Loc_3	Shen F
SDP bound	13.0%	-	-	-
FIRST/BOEM	19.3%	41	**74**	44
VOTE/BOEM	20.0%	**46**	**73**	**50**
SA	20.3%	42	**73**	45
BEST/BOEM	21.3%	43	**73**	47
BOEM	21.5%	22	72	21
PIVOT/BOEM	22.0%	**45**	72	**50**
VOTE	26.3%	44	72	48
BEST	37.1%	40	67	44
PIVOT	44.4%	39	66	44
FIRST	58.3%	39	62	41

Additive Weights				
	Obj	1-1	Loc_3	Shen F
SDP bound	16.2%	-	-	-
FIRST/BOEM	21.7%	40	**73**	44
BOEM	22.3%	22	**73**	20
BEST/BOEM	22.7%	44	**74**	**49**
VOTE/BOEM	23.3%	**46**	**73**	**50**
SA	23.8%	41	72	46
PIVOT/BOEM	24.8%	**46**	73	**50**
VOTE	30.5%	44	71	**49**
EC '08	-	41	**73**	44
BEST	42.1%	43	69	47
PIVOT	48.4%	38	67	44
FIRST	69.0%	40	59	41

Table 3: Score of the solution with best objective found by each solver on the chat test dataset, averaged over 6 annotations, sorted by objective.

	Num clusters
Max human annotator	*128*
PIVOT	122
VOTE	99
PIVOT/BOEM	89
VOTE/BOEM	86
Mean human annotator	*81*
BEST	70
FIRST	70
Elsner and Charniak (2008)	*63*
BEST/BOEM	62
SA	57
FIRST/BOEM	54
Min human annotator	*50*
BOEM	7

Table 4: Average number of clusters found (using additive weights) for chat test data.

	1-1	Loc_3	Shen F
Log-wt	-.40	-.68	-.35
Top 10 %	.14	-.15	.15
Add-wt	-.31	-.67	-.25
Top 10 %	-.07	-.22	.13

Table 5: Kendall's tau correlation between objective and metric values for the chat test set, for all solutions and top 10% of solutions.

Whatever algorithm is used to provide an initial solution, we advise the use of local search as a post-process. BOEM always improves both objective and metric values over its starting point.

The objective value is not always sufficient to select a good solution (as in the chat dataset). If possible, experimenters should check statistics like the number of clusters found to make sure they conform roughly to expectations. Algorithms that find far too many or too few clusters, regardless of objective, are unlikely to be useful. This type of problem can be especially dangerous if the pairwise classifier abstains for many pairs of points.

SDP provides much tighter bounds than the trivial bound used in previous work, although how much tighter varies with dataset (about 12 times smaller for newsgroups, 3 times for chat). This bound can be used to evaluate the absolute performance of our solvers; the VOTE/BOEM solver whose use we recommend is within about 5% of optimality. Some of this 5% represents the difference between the bound and optimality; the rest is the difference between the optimum and the solution found. If the bound were exactly optimal, we could expect a significant improvement on our best results, but not a very large one—especially since correlation between objective and metric values grows weaker for the best solutions. While it might be useful to investigate more sophisticated local searches in an attempt to close the gap, we do not view this as a priority.

Acknowledgements

We thank Christoph Helmberg, Claire Mathieu and three reviewers.

References

Nir Ailon, Moses Charikar, and Alantha Newman. 2008. Aggregating inconsistent information: Ranking and clustering. *Journal of the ACM*, 55(5):Article No. 23.

Nikhil Bansal, Avrim Blum, and Shuchi Chawla. 2004. Correlation clustering. *Machine Learning*, 56(1-3):89–113.

Regina Barzilay and Mirella Lapata. 2006. Aggregation via set partitioning for natural language generation. In *HLT-NAACL*.

Amir Ben-Dor, Ron Shamir, and Zohar Yakhini. 1999. Clustering gene expression patterns. *Journal of Computational Biology*, 6(3-4):281–297.

Michael Bertolacci and Anthony Wirth. 2007. Are approximation algorithms for consensus clustering worthwhile? In *SDM '07: Procs. 7th SIAM International Conference on Data Mining*.

Moses Charikar, Venkatesan Guruswami, and Anthony Wirth. 2005. Clustering with qualitative information. *J. Comput. Syst. Sci.*, 71(3):360–383.

William W. Cohen and Jacob Richman. 2002. Learning to match and cluster large high-dimensional data sets for data integration. In *KDD '02*, pages 475–480. ACM.

Scott Deerwester, Susan T. Dumais, George W. Furnas, Thomas K. Landauer, and Richard Harshman. 1990. Indexing by latent semantic analysis. *Journal of the American Society for Information Science*, 41:391–407.

Erik D. Demaine, Dotan Emanuel, Amos Fiat, and Nicole Immorlica. 2006. Correlation clustering in general weighted graphs. *Theor. Comput. Sci.*, 361(2):172–187.

Micha Elsner and Eugene Charniak. 2008. You talking to me? a corpus and algorithm for conversation disentanglement. In *Proceedings of ACL-08: HLT*, pages 834–842, Columbus, Ohio, June. Association for Computational Linguistics.

Jenny Rose Finkel and Christopher D. Manning. 2008. Enforcing transitivity in coreference resolution. In *Proceedings of ACL-08: HLT, Short Papers*, pages 45–48, Columbus, Ohio, June. Association for Computational Linguistics.

Aristides Gionis, Heikki Mannila, and Panayiotis Tsaparas. 2007. Clustering aggregation. *ACM Trans. on Knowledge Discovery from Data*, 1(1):Article 4.

Ioannis Giotis and Venkatesan Guruswami. 2006. Correlation clustering with a fixed number of clusters. *Theory of Computing*, 2(1):249–266.

Andrey Goder and Vladimir Filkov. 2008. Consensus clustering algorithms: Comparison and refinement. In *ALENEX '08: Procs. 10th Workshop on Algorithm Enginering and Experiments*, pages 109–117. SIAM.

Cristoph Helmberg. 2000. Semidefinite programming for combinatorial optimization. Technical Report ZR-00-34, Konrad-Zuse-Zentrum für Informationstechnik Berlin.

Cristoph Helmberg, 2009. *The ConicBundle Library for Convex Optimization*. Ver. 0.2i from `http://www-user.tu-chemnitz.de/~helmberg/ConicBundle/`.

Thorsten Joachims and John Hopcroft. 2005. Error bounds for correlation clustering. In *ICML '05*, pages 385–392, New York, NY, USA. ACM.

Thorsten Joachims. 1997. A probabilistic analysis of the Rocchio algorithm with TFIDF for text categorization. In *International Conference on Machine Learning (ICML)*, pages 143–151.

Igor Malioutov and Regina Barzilay. 2006. Minimum cut model for spoken lecture segmentation. In *ACL*. The Association for Computer Linguistics.

Claire Mathieu and Warren Schudy. 2008. Correlation clustering with noisy input. Unpublished manuscript available from http://www.cs.brown.edu/~ws/papers/clustering.pdf.

Andrew McCallum and Ben Wellner. 2004. Conditional models of identity uncertainty with application to noun coreference. In *Proceedings of the 18th Annual Conference on Neural Information Processing Systems (NIPS)*, pages 905–912. MIT Press.

Marina Meila. 2007. Comparing clusterings–an information based distance. *Journal of Multivariate Analysis*, 98(5):873–895, May.

Vincent Ng and Claire Cardie. 2002. Improving machine learning approaches to coreference resolution. In *Proceedings of the 40th Annual Meeting of the Association for Computational Linguistics*, pages 104–111.

Dou Shen, Qiang Yang, Jian-Tao Sun, and Zheng Chen. 2006. Thread detection in dynamic text message streams. In *SIGIR '06*, pages 35–42, New York, NY, USA. ACM.

Wee Meng Soon, Hwee Tou Ng, and Daniel Chung Yong Lim. 2001. A machine learning approach to coreference resolution of noun phrases. *Computational Linguistics*, 27(4):521–544.

Lidan Wang and Douglas W. Oard. 2009. Context-based message expansion for disentanglement of interleaved text conversations. In *Proceedings of NAACL-09 (to appear)*.

Shi Zhong and Joydeep Ghosh. 2003. Model-based clustering with soft balancing. In *ICDM '03: Proceedings of the Third IEEE International Conference on Data Mining*, page 459, Washington, DC, USA. IEEE Computer Society.

A New Objective Function for Word Alignment

Tugba Bodrumlu **Kevin Knight** **Sujith Ravi**
Information Sciences Institute & Computer Science Department
University of Southern California
bodrumlu@usc.edu, knight@isi.edu, sravi@isi.edu

Abstract

We develop a new objective function for word alignment that measures the size of the bilingual dictionary induced by an alignment. A word alignment that results in a small dictionary is preferred over one that results in a large dictionary. In order to search for the alignment that minimizes this objective, we cast the problem as an integer linear program. We then extend our objective function to align corpora at the sub-word level, which we demonstrate on a small Turkish-English corpus.

1 Introduction

Word alignment is the problem of annotating a bilingual text with links connecting words that have the same meanings. Figure 1 shows sample input for a word aligner (Knight, 1997). After analyzing the text, we may conclude, for example, that *sprok* corresponds to *dat* in the first sentence pair.

Word alignment has several downstream consumers. One is machine translation, where programs extract translation rules from word-aligned corpora (Och and Ney, 2004; Galley et al., 2004; Chiang, 2007; Quirk et al., 2005). Other downstream processes exploit dictionaries derived by alignment, in order to translate queries in cross-lingual IR (Schönhofen et al., 2008) or re-score candidate translation outputs (Och et al., 2004).

Many methods of automatic alignment have been proposed. Probabilistic generative models like IBM 1-5 (Brown et al., 1993), HMM (Vogel et al., 1996), ITG (Wu, 1997), and LEAF (Fraser and Marcu, 2007) define formulas for P(f | e) or P(e, f), with

ok-voon ororok sprok
at-voon bichat dat

erok sprok izok hihok ghirok
totat dat arrat vat hilat

ok-drubel ok-voon anok plok sprok
at-drubel at-voon pippat rrat dat

ok-voon anok drok brok jok
at-voon krat pippat sat lat

wiwok farok izok stok
totat jjat quat cat

lalok sprok izok jok stok
wat dat krat quat cat

lalok farok ororok lalok sprok izok enemok
wat jjat bichat wat dat vat eneat

lalok brok anok plok nok
iat lat pippat rrat nnat

wiwok nok izok kantok ok-yurp
totat nnat quat oloat at-yurp

lalok mok nok yorok ghirok clok
wat nnat gat mat bat hilat

lalok nok crrrok hihok yorok zanzanok
wat nnat arrat mat zanzanat

lalok rarok nok izok hihok mok
wat nnat forat arrat vat gat

Figure 1: Word alignment exercise (Knight, 1997).

Proceedings of the NAACL HLT Workshop on Integer Linear Programming for Natural Language Processing, pages 28–35,
Boulder, Colorado, June 2009.

hidden alignment variables. EM algorithms estimate dictionary and other probabilities in order to maximize those quantities. One can then ask for Viterbi alignments that maximize P(alignment | e, f). Discriminative models, e.g. (Taskar et al., 2005), instead set parameters to maximize alignment accuracy against a hand-aligned development set. EMD training (Fraser and Marcu, 2006) combines generative and discriminative elements.

Low accuracy is a weakness for all systems. Most practitioners still use 1990s algorithms to align their data. It stands to reason that we have not yet seen the last word in alignment models.

In this paper, we develop a new objective function for alignment, inspired by watching people manually solve the alignment exercise of Figure 1. When people attack this problem, we find that once they create a bilingual dictionary entry, they like to *reuse* that entry as much as possible. Previous machine aligners emulate this to some degree, but they are not explicitly programmed to do so.

We also address another weakness of current aligners: they only align full words. With few exceptions, e.g. (Zhang et al., 2003; Snyder and Barzilay, 2008), aligners do not operate at the sub-word level, making them much less useful for agglutinative languages such as Turkish.

Our present contributions are as follows:

- We offer a simple new objective function that scores a corpus alignment based on how many distinct bilingual word pairs it contains.
- We use an integer programming solver to carry out optimization and corpus alignment.
- We extend the system to perform subword alignment, which we demonstrate on a Turkish-English corpus.

The results in this paper constitute a proof of concept of these ideas, executed on small corpora. We conclude by listing future directions.

2 New Objective Function for Alignment

We search for the legal alignment that *minimizes the size of the induced bilingual dictionary*. By dictionary size, we mean the number of distinct word-pairs linked in the corpus alignment. We can immediately investigate how different alignments stack up, according to this objective function. Figure 2

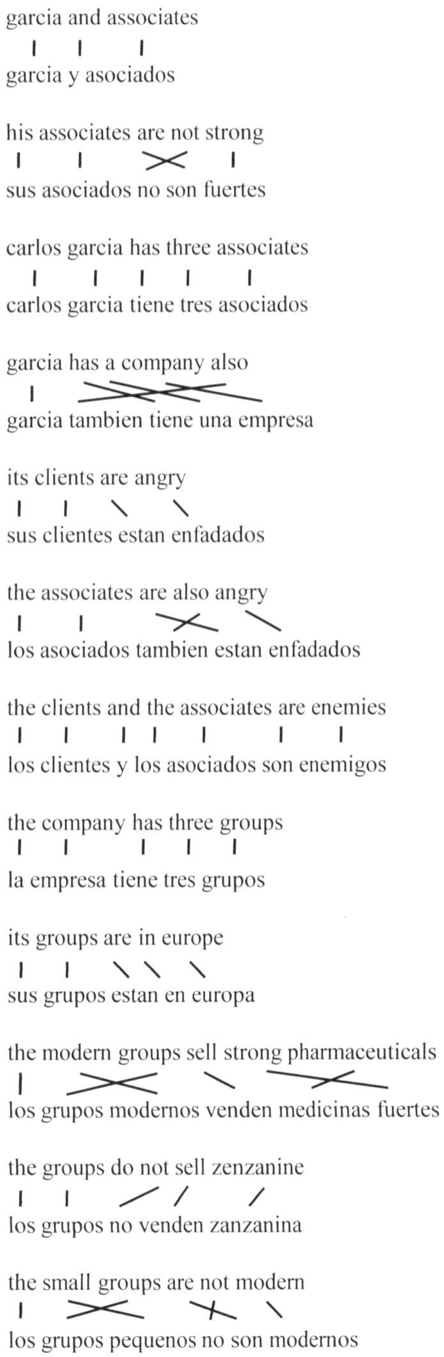

Figure 2: Gold alignment. The induced bilingual dictionary has 28 distinct entries, including garcia/garcia, are/son, are/estan, not/no, has/tiene, etc.

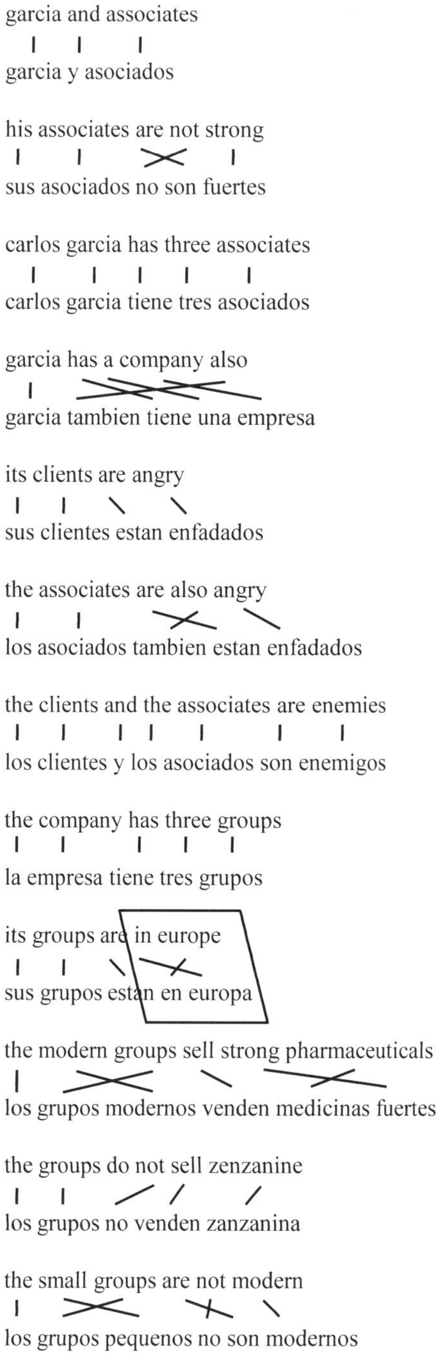

Figure 3: IP alignment. The induced bilingual dictionary has 28 distinct entries.

shows the gold alignment for the corpus in Figure 1 (displayed here as English-Spanish), which results in 28 distinct bilingual dictionary entries. By contrast, a monotone alignment induces 39 distinct entries, due to less re-use.

Next we look at how to automatically rifle through all legal alignments to find the one with the best score. What is a legal alignment? For now, we consider it to be one where:

- Every foreign word is aligned exactly once (Brown et al., 1993).
- Every English word has either 0 or 1 alignments (Melamed, 1997).

We formulate our integer program (IP) as follows. We set up two types of binary variables:

- Alignment link variables. If *link-i-j-k* = 1, that means in sentence pair i, the foreign word at position j aligns to the English words at position k.
- Bilingual dictionary variables. If *dict-f-e* = 1, that means word pair (f, e) is "in" the dictionary.

We constrain the values of *link* variables to satisfy the two alignment conditions listed earlier. We also require that if *link-i-j-k* = 1 (i.e., we've decided on an alignment link), then $\textit{dict-}f_{ij}\textit{-}e_{ik}$ should also equal 1 (the linked words are recorded as a dictionary entry).[1] We do not require the converse—just because a word pair is available in the dictionary, the aligner does not have to link every instance of that word pair. For example, if an English sentence has two *the* tokens, and its Spanish translation has two *la* tokens, we should not require that all four links be active—in fact, this would conflict with the 1-1 *link* constraints and render the integer program unsolvable. The IP reads as follows:

minimize:
$\sum_{f,e} \textit{dict-f-e}$
subject to:
$\forall_{i,j} \sum_k \textit{link-i-j-k} = 1$
$\forall_{i,k} \sum_j \textit{link-i-j-k} \leq 1$
$\forall_{i,j,k}\ \textit{link-i-j-k} \leq \textit{dict-}f_{ij}\textit{-}e_{ik}$

On our Spanish-English corpus, the *cplex*[2] solver obtains a minimal objective function value of 28. To

[1] f_{ij} is the jth foreign word in the ith sentence pair.
[2] www.ilog.com/products/cplex

get the second-best alignment, we add a constraint to our IP requiring the sum of the n variables active in the previous solution to be less than n, and we re-run *cplex*. This forces *cplex* to choose different variable settings on the second go-round. We repeat this procedure to get an ordered list of alignments.[3]

We find that there are 8 distinct solutions that yield the same objective function value of 28. Figure 3 shows one of these. This alignment is not bad, considering that word-order information is not encoded in the IP. We can now compare several alignments in terms of both dictionary size and alignment accuracy. For accuracy, we represent each alignment as a set of tuples $< i, j, k >$, where i is the sentence pair, j is a foreign index, and k is an English index. We use these tuples to calculate a balanced f-score against the gold alignment tuples.[4]

Method	Dict size	f-score
Gold	28	100.0
Monotone	39	68.9
IBM-1 (Brown et al., 1993)	30	80.3
IBM-4 (Brown et al., 1993)	29	86.9
IP	28	95.9

The last line shows an average f-score over the 8 tied IP solutions.

Figure 4 further investigates the connection between our objective function and alignment accuracy. We sample up to 10 alignments at each of several objective function values v, by first adding a constraint that *dict* variables add to exactly v, then iterating the n-best list procedure above. We stop when we have 10 solutions, or when *cplex* fails to find another solution with value v. In this figure, we see a clear relationship between the objective function and alignment accuracy—minimizing the former is a good way to maximize the latter.

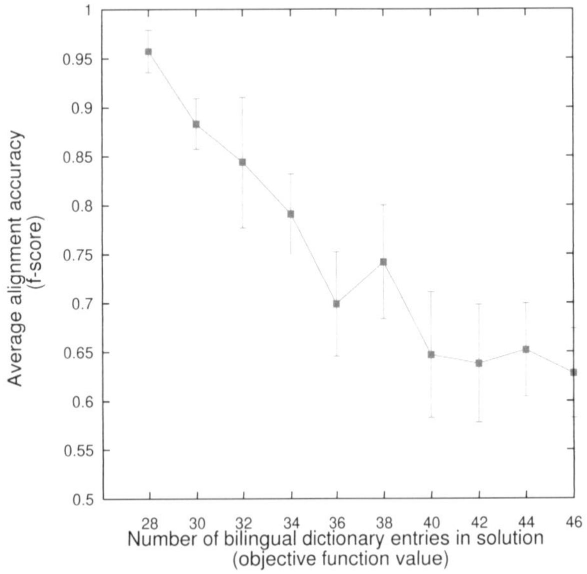

Figure 4: Relationship between IP objective (x-axis = size of induced bilingual dictionary) and alignment accuracy (y-axis = f-score).

Turkish	**English**
yururum	i walk
yururler	they walk

Figure 5: Two Turkish-English sentence pairs.

3 Sub-Word Alignment

We now turn to alignment at the sub-word level. Agglutinative languages like Turkish present challenges for many standard NLP techniques. An agglutinative language can express in a single word (e.g., *yurumuyoruz*) what might require many words in another language (e.g., *we are not walking*). Naively breaking on whitespace results in a very large vocabulary for Turkish, and it ignores the multi-morpheme structure inside Turkish words.

Consider the tiny Turkish-English corpus in Figure 5. Even a non-Turkish speaker might plausibly align *yurur* to *walk*, *um* to *I*, and *ler* to *they*. However, none of the popular machine aligners is able to do this, since they align at the whole-word level. Designers of translation systems sometimes employ language-specific word breakers before alignment, though these are hard to build and maintain, and they are usually not only language-specific, but also language-pair-specific. Good un-

[3]This method not only suppresses the IP solutions generated so far, but it suppresses additional solutions as well. In particular, it suppresses solutions in which all *link* and *dict* variables have the same values as in some previous solution, but some additional *dict* variables are flipped to 1. We consider this a feature rather than a bug, as it ensures that all alignments in the n-best list are unique. For what we report in this paper, we only create n-best lists whose elements possess the same objective function value, so the issue does not arise.

[4]P = proportion of proposed links that are in gold, R = proportion of gold links that are proposed, and f-score = 2PR/(P+R).

supervised monolingual morpheme segmenters are also available (Goldsmith, 2001; Creutz and Lagus, 2005), though again, these do not do joint inference of alignment and word segmentation.

We extend our objective function straightforwardly to sub-word alignment. To test our extension, we construct a Turkish-English corpus of 1616 sentence pairs. We first manually construct a regular tree grammar (RTG) (Gecseg and Steinby, 1984) for a fragment of English. This grammar produces English trees; it has 86 rules, 26 states, and 53 terminals (English words). We then construct a tree-to-string transducer (Rounds, 1970) that converts English trees into Turkish *character* strings, including space. Because it does not explicitly enumerate the Turkish vocabulary, this transducer can output a very large number of distinct Turkish words (i.e., character sequences preceded and followed by space). This transducer has 177 rules, 18 states, and 23 terminals (Turkish characters). RTG generation produces English trees that the transducer converts to Turkish, both via the tree automata toolkit Tiburon (May and Knight, 2006). From this, we obtain a parallel Turkish-English corpus. A fragment of the corpus is shown in Figure 6. Because we will concentrate on finding Turkish sub-words, we manually break off the English sub-word *-ing*, by rule, as seen in the last line of the figure.

This is a small corpus, but good for demonstrating our concept. By automatically tracing the internal operation of the tree transducer, we also produce a gold alignment for the corpus. We use the gold alignment to tabulate the number of morphemes per Turkish word:

n	% Turkish **types** with n morphemes	% Turkish **tokens** with n morphemes
1	23.1%	35.5%
2	63.5%	61.6%
3	13.4%	2.9%

Naturally, these statistics imply that standard whole-word aligners will fail. By inspecting the corpus, we find that 26.8 is the maximium f-score available to whole-word alignment methods.

Now we adjust our IP formulation. We broaden the definition of legal alignment to include breaking any foreign word (token) into one or more sub-word (tokens). Each resulting sub-word token is aligned to exactly one English word token, and every English word aligns to 0 or 1 foreign sub-words. Our *dict-f-e* variables now relate Turkish sub-words to English words. The first sentence pair in Figure 5 would have previously contributed two *dict* variables; now it contributes 44, including things like *dict-uru-walk*. We consider an alignment to be a set of tuples $< i, j1, j2, k >$, where $j1$ and $j2$ are start and end indices into the foreign character string. We create *align-i-j1-j2-k* variables that connect Turkish character spans with English word indices. Alignment variables constrain dictionary variables as before, i.e., an alignment link can only "turn on" when licensed by the dictionary.

We previously constrained every Turkish word to align to something. However, we do not want every Turkish character *span* to align—only the spans explicitly chosen in our word segmentation. So we introduce *span-i-j1-j2* variables to indicate segmentation decisions. Only when *span-i-j1-j2* = 1 do we require $\sum_k$ *align-i-j1-j2-k* = 1.

For a coherent segmentation, the set of active *span* variables must cover all Turkish letter tokens in the corpus, and no pair of spans may overlap each other. To implement these constraints, we create a lattice where each node represents a Turkish index, and each transition corresponds to a *span* variable. In a coherent segmentation, the sum of all *span* variables entering an lattice-internal node equals the sum of all *span* variables leaving that node. If the sum of all variables leaving the start node equals 1, then we are guaranteed a left-to-right path through the lattice, i.e., a coherent choice of 0 and 1 values for *span* variables.

The IP reads as follows:

minimize:
$\sum_{f,e}$ *dict-f-e*
subject to:
$\forall_{i,j1,j2} \sum_k \textit{align-i-j1-j2-k} = \textit{span-i-j1-j2}$
$\forall_{i,k} \sum_{j1,j2} \textit{align-i-j1-j2-k} \leq 1$
$\forall_{i,j1,j2,k}\ \textit{align-i-j1-j2-k} \leq \textit{dict-}f_{i,j1,j2}\textit{-}e_{i,k}$
$\forall_{i,j} \sum_{j3} \textit{span-i-j3-j} = \sum_{j3} \textit{span-i-j-j3}$
$\forall_{i,w} \sum_{j>w} \textit{span-i-w-j} = 1$
(w ranges over Turkish word start indices)

With our simple objective function, we obtain an f-score of 61.4 against the gold standard. Sample gold and IP alignments are shown in Figure 7.

Turkish	**English**
onlari gordum	i saw them
gidecekler	they will go
onu stadyumda gordum	i saw him in the stadium
ogretmenlerim tiyatroya yurudu	my teachers walked to the theatre
cocuklar yurudu	the girls walked
babam restorana gidiyor	my father is walk ing to the restaurant
...	...

Figure 6: A Turkish-English corpus produced by an English grammar pipelined with an English-to-Turkish tree-to-string transducer.

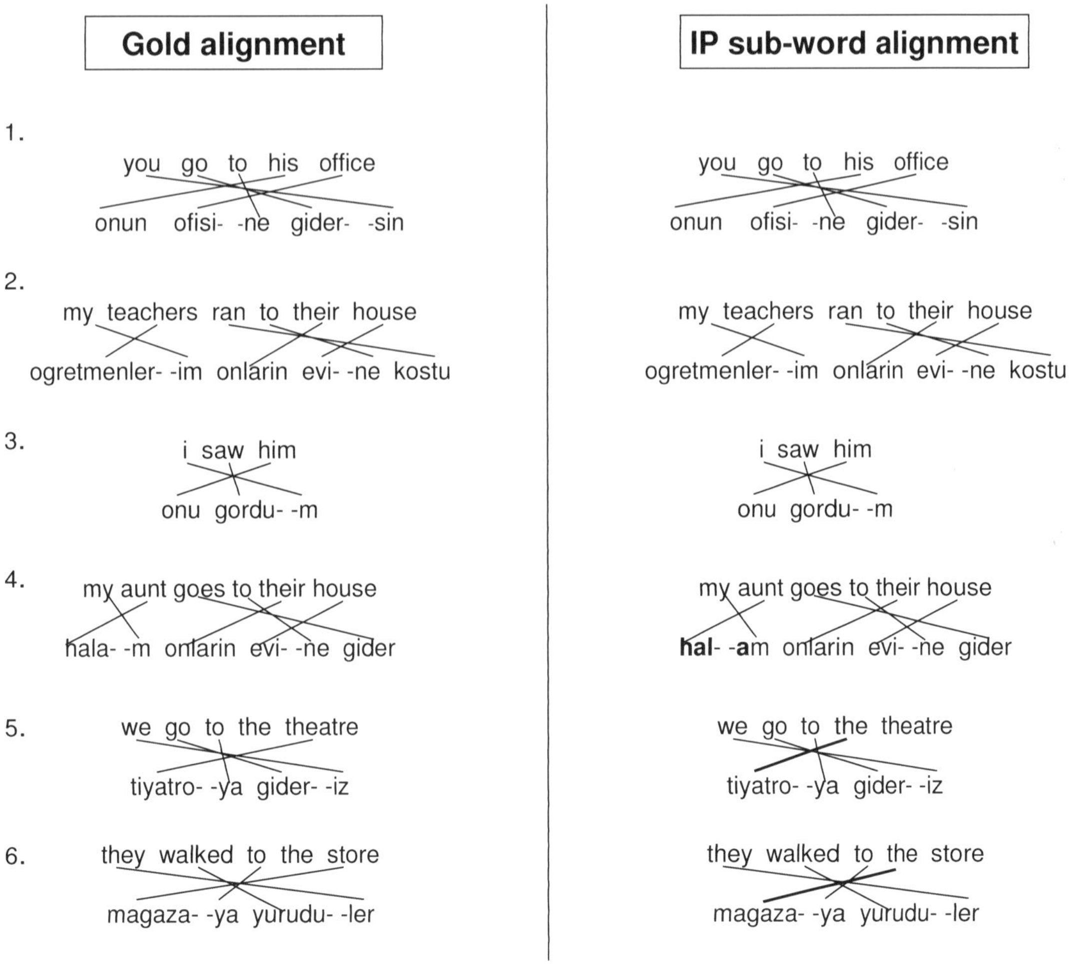

Figure 7: Sample gold and (initial) IP sub-word alignments on our Turkish-English corpus. Dashes indicate where the IP search has decided to break Turkish words in the process of aligning. For examples, the word *magazaya* has been broken into *magaza-* and *-ya*.

The last two incorrect alignments in the figure are instructive. The system has decided to align English *the* to the Turkish noun morphemes *tiyatro* and *magaza*, and to leave English nouns *theatre* and *store* unaligned. This is a tie-break decision. It is equally good for the objective function to leave *the* unaligned instead—either way, there are two relevant dictionary entries.

We fix this problem by introducing a special NULL Turkish token, and by modifying the IP to require every English token to align (either to NULL or something else). This introduces a cost for failing to align an English token x to Turkish, because a new *x/NULL* dictionary entry will have to be created. (The NULL token itself is unconstrained in how many tokens it may align to.)

Under this scheme, the last two incorrect alignments in Figure 7 induce four relevant dictionary entries (*the/tiyatro, the/magaza, theatre/NULL, store/NULL*) while the gold alignment induces only three (*the/NULL, theatre/tiyatro, store/magaza*), because *the/NULL* is re-used. The gold alignment is therefore now preferred by the IP optimizer. There is a rippling effect, causing the system to correct many other decisions as well. This revision raises the alignment f-score from 61.4 to 83.4.

The following table summarizes our alignment results. In the table, "Dict" refers to the size of the induced dictionary, and "Sub-words" refers to the number of induced Turkish sub-word tokens.

Method	Dict	Sub-words	f-score
Gold (sub-word)	67	8102	100.0
Monotone (word)	512	4851	5.5
IBM-1 (word)	220	4851	21.6
IBM-4 (word)	230	4851	20.3
IP (word)	107	4851	20.1
IP (sub-word, initial)	60	7418	61.4
IP (sub-word, revised)	65	8105	83.4

Our search for an optimal IP solution is not fast. It takes 1-5 hours to perform sub-word alignment on the Turkish-English corpus. Of course, if we wanted to obtain optimal alignments under IBM Model 4, that would also be expensive, in fact NP-complete (Raghavendra and Maji, 2006). Practical Model 4 systems therefore make substantial search approximations (Brown et al., 1993).

4 Related Work

(Zhang et al., 2003) and (Wu, 1997) tackle the problem of segmenting Chinese while aligning it to English. (Snyder and Barzilay, 2008) use multilingual data to compute segmentations of Arabic, Hebrew, Aramaic, and English. Their method uses IBM models to bootstrap alignments, and they measure the resulting segmentation accuracy.

(Taskar et al., 2005) cast their alignment model as a minimum cost quadratic flow problem, for which optimal alignments can be computed with off-the-shelf optimizers. Alignment in the modified model of (Lacoste-Julien et al., 2006) can be mapped to a quadratic assignment problem and solved with linear programming tools. In that work, linear programming is not only used for alignment, but also for training weights for the discriminative model. These weights are trained on a manually-aligned subset of the parallel data. One important "mega" feature for the discriminative model is the score assigned by an IBM model, which must be separately trained on the full parallel data. Our work differs in two ways: (1) our training is unsupervised, requiring no manually aligned data, and (2) we do not bootstrap off IBM models. (DeNero and Klein, 2008) gives an integer linear programming formulation of another alignment model based on phrases. There, integer programming is used only for alignment, not for learning parameter values.

5 Conclusions and Future Work

We have presented a novel objective function for alignment, and we have applied it to whole-word and sub-word alignment problems. Preliminary results look good, especially given that new objective function is simpler than those previously proposed. The integer programming framework makes the model easy to implement, and its optimal behavior frees us from worrying about search errors.

We believe there are good future possibilities for this work:

- **Extend legal alignments to cover n-to-m and discontinuous cases**. While morpheme-to-morpheme alignment is more frequently a

1-to-1 affair than word-to-word alignment is, the 1-to-1 assumption is not justified in either case.

- **Develop new components for the IP objective**. Our current objective function makes no reference to word order, so if the same word appears twice in a sentence, a tie-break ensues.
- **Establish complexity bounds for optimizing dictionary size**. We conjecture that optimal alignment according to our model is NP-complete in the size of the corpus.
- **Develop a fast, approximate alignment algorithm for our model**.
- **Test on large-scale bilingual corpora**.

Acknowledgments

This work was partially supported under DARPA GALE, Contract No. HR0011-06-C-0022.

References

P. Brown, V. Della Pietra, S. Della Pietra, and R. Mercer. 1993. The mathematics of statistical machine translation: Parameter estimation. *Computational linguistics*, 19(2).

D. Chiang. 2007. Hierarchical phrase-based translation. *Computational Linguistics*, 33(2).

M. Creutz and K. Lagus. 2005. Inducing the morphological lexicon of a natural language from unannotated text. In *Proc. AKRR*.

J. DeNero and D. Klein. 2008. The complexity of phrase alignment problems. In *Proc. ACL*.

A. Fraser and D. Marcu. 2006. Semi-supervised training for statistical word alignment. In *Proc. ACL-COLING*.

A. Fraser and D. Marcu. 2007. Getting the structure right for word alignment: LEAF. In *Proc. EMNLP-CoNLL*.

M. Galley, M. Hopkins, K. Knight, and D Marcu. 2004. What's in a translation rule. In *Proc. NAACL-HLT*.

F. Gecseg and M. Steinby. 1984. *Tree automata*. Akademiai Kiado.

J. Goldsmith. 2001. Unsupervised learning of the morphology of a natural language. *Computational Linguistics*, 27(2).

K. Knight. 1997. Automating knowledge acquisition for machine translation. *AI Magazine*, 18(4).

S. Lacoste-Julien, B. Taskar, D. Klein, and M. Jordan. 2006. Word alignment via quadratic assignment. In *Proc. HLT-NAACL*.

J. May and K. Knight. 2006. Tiburon: A weighted tree automata toolkit. In *Proc. CIAA*.

I. D. Melamed. 1997. A word-to-word model of translational equivalence. In *Proc. ACL*.

F. J. Och and H. Ney. 2004. The alignment template approach to statistical machine translation. *Computational Linguistics*, 30(4).

F. J. Och, D. Gildea, S. Khudanpur, A. Sarkar, K. Yamada, A. Fraser, S. Kumar, L. Shen, D. Smith, K. Eng, V. Jain, Z. Jin, and D. Radev. 2004. A smorgasbord of features for statistical machine translation. In *Proc. HLT-NAACL*.

C. Quirk, A. Menezes, and C. Cherry. 2005. Dependency treelet translation: Syntactically informed phrasal SMT. In *Proc. ACL*.

U. Raghavendra and H. K. Maji. 2006. Computational complexity of statistical machine translation. In *Proc. EACL*.

W. Rounds. 1970. Mappings and grammars on trees. *Theory of Computing Systems*, 4(3).

P. Schönhofen, A. Benczúr, I. Bíró, and K. Csalogány, 2008. *Cross-language retrieval with wikipedia*. Springer.

B. Snyder and R. Barzilay. 2008. Unsupervised multilingual learning for morphological segmentation. In *Proc. ACL*.

B. Taskar, S. Lacoste-Julien, and D. Klein. 2005. A discriminative matching approach to word alignment. In *Proc. EMNLP*.

S. Vogel, H. Ney, and C. Tillmann. 1996. HMM-based word alignment in statistical translation. In *Proc. ACL*.

D. Wu. 1997. Stochastic inversion transduction grammars and bilingual parsing of parallel corpora. *Computational Linguistics*, 23(3).

Y. Zhang, S. Vogel, and A. Waibel. 2003. Integrated phrase segmentation and alignment algorithm for statistical machine translation. In *Proc. Intl. Conf. on NLP and KE*.

A Constraint Programming Approach to Probabilistic Syntactic Processing

Irene Langkilde-Geary
Independent Consultant
South Jordan, UT USA
i.l.geary@gmail.com

1 Introduction

Integer linear programming (ILP) is a framework for solving combinatorial problems with linear constraints of the form $y = c_1x_1 + c_2x_2 + ... + c_nx_n$ where the variables (ie., y and x_is) take on only integer values. ILP is a special case of a larger family of contraint-based solving techniques in which variables may take on additional types of values (eg. discrete, symbolic, real, set, and structured) or involve additional kinds of constraints (eg. logical and non-linear, such as $x \wedge y \Rightarrow z$ and $y = cx^n$). Constraint-based problem solving approaches offer a more natural way of modeling many kinds of real-world problems. Furthermore, the declarative nature of constraint-based approaches makes them versatile since the order in which the variables are solved is not predetermined. The same program can thus be reused for solving different subsets of the problem's variables. Additionally, in some cases, constraint-based approaches can solve problems more efficiently or accurately than alternative approaches.

Constraint Programming (CP) is a field of research that develops algorithms and tools for constraint-based problem solving. This abstract describes work-in-progress on a project to develop a CP-based general-purpose broad-coverage probabilistic syntactic language processing system for English. Because of its declarative nature, the system can be used for both parsing and realization as well as their subtasks (such as tagging, chunk parsing, lexical choice, or word ordering) or hybridizations (like text-to-text generation). We expect this tool to be useful for a wide range of applications from information extraction to machine translation to human-computer dialog. An ambitious project such as this poses a number of questions and difficult challenges, including: a) how to declaratively represent the syntactic structure of sentences, b) how to integrate the processing of hard constraints with soft (probabilistic) ones, c) how to overcome problems of intractibility associated with large problems and rich representations in learning, inference, as well as search.

2 Related Work

Declarative and constraint-based representations and computation mechanisms have been the subject of much research in the fields of both Linguistics and Computer Science over the last 30-40 years, at times motivating each other but also sometimes developing independently. Although there is quite a large literature on constraint-based processing in NLP, the notion of a constraint and the methods for processing them vary significantly from that in CP. See (Duchier et al., 1998; Piwek and van Deemter, 2006; Blache, 2000). The CP approach has been designed for a broader ranger of applications and rests on a stronger, more general theoretical foundation. It coherently integrates a variety of solving techniques whereas theoretical linguistic formalisms have traditionally used only a single kind of constraint solver, namely unification. In comparison, the 2009 ILPNLP workshop focuses on NLP processing using solely integer linear constraints.

Proceedings of the NAACL HLT Workshop on Integer Linear Programming for Natural Language Processing, pages 36–37,
Boulder, Colorado, June 2009.

3 Methodology

Three key elements of our approach are its syntactic representation, confidence-based beam search, and a novel on-demand learning and inference algorithm. The last is used to calculate probability-based feature costs and the confidences used to heuristically guide the search for the best solution. A description of the flat featurized dependency-style syntactic representation we use is available in (Langkilde-Geary and Betteridge, 2006), which describes how the entire Penn Treebank (Marcus et al., 1993) was converted to this representation. The representation has been designed to offer finer-grained declarativeness than other existing representations.

Our confidence-based search heuristic evaluates the conditional likelihood of undetermined output variables (ie., word features) at each step of search and heuristically selects the case of the mostly likely variable/value pair as the next (or only one) to explore. The likelihood is contextualized by the input variables and any output variables which have already been explored and tentatively solved. Although one theoretical advantage of CP (and ILP) is the ability to calculate an overall optimal solution through search, we unexpectedly found that our confidence-based heuristic led to the first intermediate solution typically being the optimal. This allowed us to simplify the search methodology to a one-best or threshold-based beam search without any significant loss in accuracy. The result is dramatically improved scalability.

We use the concurrent CP language Mozart/Oz to implement our approach. We previously implemented an exploratory prototype that used raw frequencies instead of smoothed probabilities for the feature costs and search heuristic confidences. (Langkilde-Geary, 2005; Langkilde-Geary, 2007). The lack of smoothing severely limited the applicability of the prototype. We are currently finishing development of the before-mentioned on-demand learning algorithm which will overcome that challenge and allow us to evaluate our approach's accuracy and efficiency on a variety of NLP tasks on common test sets. Informal preliminary results on the much-studied subtask of part-of-speech tagging indicate that our method outperforms a Naive Bayes-based baseline in terms of accuracy and within 2% of state-of-the-art single-classifier methods, while running in linear time with respect to the number of output variables or word tokens. We are not aware of any other approach that achieves this level of accuracy in comparable algorithmic time.

4 Conclusion

The versatility and potential scalability of our approach are its most noteworthy aspects. We expect it to be able to handle not only a wider variety of NLP tasks than existing approaches but also to tackle harder tasks that have been intractible before now. Although ILP has the same theoretical power as CP for efficiently solving problems, our approach takes advantage of several capabilities that CP offers that ILP doesn't, including modeling with not only linear constraints but also logical, set-based and other kinds of constraints; customized search methodology with dynamically computed costs, and conditionally applied constraints, among others.

References

P. Blache. 2000. Constraints, linguistic theories and natural language processing. *Natural Language Processing*, 1835.

D. Duchier, C. Gardent, and J. Niehren. 1998. Concurrent constraint programming in oz for natural language processing. Technical report, Universitt des Saarlandes.

I. Langkilde-Geary and J. Betteridge. 2006. A factored functional dependency transformation of the english penn treebank for probabilistic surface generation. In *Proc. LREC*.

I. Langkilde-Geary. 2005. An exploratory application of constraint optimization in mozart to probabilistic natural language processing. In H. Christiansen, P. Skadhauge, and J. Villadsen, editors, *Proceedings of the International Workshop on Constraint Solving and Language Processing (CSLP)*, volume 3438. Springer-Verlag LNAI.

I. Langkilde-Geary. 2007. Declarative syntactic processing of natural language using concurrent constraint programming and probabilistic dependency modeling. In *Proc. UCNLG*.

M. Marcus, B. Santorini, and M. Marcinkiewicz. 1993. Building a large annotated corpus of english: the Penn treebank. *Computational Linguistics*, 19(2).

P. Piwek and K. van Deemter. 2006. Constraint-based natural language generation: A survey. Technical report, The Open University.